To Linda with love and respect. Irene Davon

Failure Is Not An Option

Cover art painted by Irene Danon.

Prepared for publication, edited and cover designed by JoDee Vale.

DEDICATION

This book is dedicated to Dr. Ruth Gruber,
who risked her own life to save ours.
She made her way to Europe,
in the middle of Hell of World War II
and brought us to safety
and a new life in the United States.
She was the mother,
who took her child by the hand
and gave him life and love.

ACKNOWLEDGEMENTS

This book is also dedicated to my daughter Michelle,
or as we call her, my third eye.

INTRODUCTION

I had to write this book to erase any doubts about the Holocaust not happening. I was there. I lived it. I survived it, and am here to tell about it.

The fear that an eleven year old child experiences never goes away. And today, at 82 years of age, I still get a lump in my throat remembering when the Nazis took my father from us.

The pain from loss of the entire family is only equaled by the loneliness during the holidays. No nieces or nephews. No cousins. No relatives. No grandparents. Only emptiness. And then the guilt sets in to fill the vacuum. Why did I survive when they all perished?

Questioning God has become a daily chore. Why did God save me? Is there a God? Was this all at random? Did God allow the Holocaust to happen?

Even though I don't have the answers, I did try to make sense of some of the events in this book.

And when I went into real estate, I knew that if I did a good job the commissions would follow. I knew that God saved me to be an ambassador of love and to do His job. My real estate was my service to God. And that is why I

performed my service from love and not greed.

I live in gratitude. I love these United States. But more than that, I have always tried to be a good person. I have tried to give back the love, the wealth and the prosperity that this country afforded me. I love singing the Star Spangled Banner. I honor and respect this country.

God Bless America!!!!!

Index

Chapter 1 ~ Rude Awakening Page 1

Chapter 2 ~ Farm Revisited Page 13

Chapter 3 ~ The Marching Boots Page 27

Chapter 4 ~ Death Camp At Sajmishte Page 45

Chapter 5 ~ The Run Page 57

Chapter 6 ~ The Chase Page 73

Chapter 7 ~ Mostar On River Neretva Page 87

Chapter 8 ~ Surviving Is A Job Page 107

Chapter 9 ~ Bari, Italia Page 129

Chapter 10 ~ The Henry Gibbons Page 143

Chapter 11 ~ Fort Ontario Page 155

Appendix

Chapter 1

RUDE AWAKENING

I was awakened by my own screams, and before I was fully awake, my father was already standing by my bedside. His arms were outstretched as he grabbed me off my bed. The room was full of dust, shattered glass and cement that fell off the ceiling. I was numb with fear. I was 11 yrs old, and it was April 6th, 1941 and Germany had just invaded Yugoslavia. It was the beginning of World War II. Belgrade was supposed to be an open city, like Rome, but Germany ignored all previous agreements and bombed Belgrade with all its might.

In the hallway of our house, we met with my mother who was holding my seven year old brother, Ike, very tightly, his little hands clutching onto her for dear life. The sirens were screeching and the house was shaking. My parents, with their precious cargoes, ran to the basement of our house where we all nestled among the burlap sacks of potatoes, onions, and barrels of fermented cabbage. Every fall, my mother, with the maid, would fill up a barrel, a wooden keg, with cabbages and put in a ton of different spices, herbs and salt, and close it tightly. In a

few weeks we had the most delicious sauerkraut. And of course, we stored potatoes and onions in the burlap sacks for the whole winter.

My mother, Rachel, was petite and very pretty. She had all her clothes made by a seamstress, copied from a French magazine. But this morning, her black hair was messy and she looked older, in her black cashmere coat over a pink, silk nightgown.

The bombing seemed endless. I sat in my father's lap in the basement and turned my head so I could look at my brother. He was still. He was quiet. I reached and touched him. I thought he might be dead. My mother yelled at me to be still.

War Through the Eyes of a Child

What is happening, Daddy?
I am scared of bombs.
Is someone trying to kill us, Daddy?
The noise is awful.
Is our house going to
fall on us and bury us?

Why do people hate us, Daddy?
They don't even know us.
Was I a bad girl, Daddy?
I promise, I will be good.
Just make them go away.
I am very scared, Daddy.

They stopped. The noise stopped.
Can I go out and play?
I can't breathe. I am choking.
The air is so dusty.
Look Daddy, there is a hand and a leg.
Where is the person, Daddy?

Are you afraid, Daddy?
Are you scared we are going to die?
Is God taking a nap? Daddy?
You said God will take care of us.
You promised. You promised.
Where is God, Daddy?

As soon as the bombing subsided, we ran upstairs and changed out of our nightwear.

"Hurry up," my father urged. " We have to get out of here."

"Can I take some things?" I cried.

No one listened to me. So I took my mother's terrycloth robe with large pockets and put it on. It dragged on the floor. I didn't care. It had big pockets, and I started collecting things. I remember taking an alarm clock. I took a doll and put it in my pocket as well. A few cookies. I have to have some cookies. I was grabbing things and shoving them furiously into my bulging pockets. I was so concerned with what else I had to have, that I didn't realize that my parents and Ike were ready to leave the house. Suddenly I felt my father's arms grab me and lift me in the air, with the robe, pockets and all.

"What are you doing in that robe?" my father asked me in an excited voice. Both my parents stripped me of the robe and all my possessions. My mom handed Dad an old dress of mine, which he slipped over my head. Mom was dressed and holding my brother. All my father took was the cash he had on hand.

The sun had just come out. The street was lined with dust, flying papers, plaster, cement bricks, and bodies. There were dead bodies everywhere. People were running in all directions. We ran south. We stopped. We turned around, and ran north. No one knew where they were going. Suddenly my father yelled out, "The post office. We are going to the post office."

The post office was a fairly new, nine-story building, and it was built with steel and stone. We ran through the streets, cluttered with fallen bricks and dead bodies. As we approached the building, we were pushed and rushed, as the mob of the entire city tried to get into the post office building.

The sirens started again. We pushed our way through hundreds of people to the basement, which served as a shelter. It was semi-dark and it felt damp. Both my parents, still holding us, sat down on the damp floor, which was already lined with people. Children were screaming with fright, and most of the adults prayed, some softly and some screaming at God.

"Shema Israel!"
"Help me, Jesus!"
"God help us all!"

Those were some of the cries that emerged from the sea of bodies huddled on the cold cement floor. It seemed that each person reached across his own bridge of faith to his own personal god, asking for help. The bombing lasted for an hour and a half, resulting in 4000 deaths.

My ears were hurting. I was a sickly child and had all the childhood diseases, like Scarlet Fever, Diphtheria, Whooping Cough and Measles. Doctors didn't think I was going to see my fifth birthday. My immune system was poor, which reflected in my health. In order to preserve the little health I had, my parents bought me a white lamb, which became my only friend. So Josefina, our maid, a little lamb, and I became a regular sight in the gorgeous park of Kalimegdan, the largest and most

beautiful park in Belgrade. I loved looking at all the statues which adorned the grounds.

The very high fever, from Diphtheria, burned my throat and my tonsils and left me almost deaf in my left ear. The doctor said that my eardrum fell out of place, or something like that. The only way to correct that situation was with surgery, which was scheduled, but preempted by the war.

I could hear the sirens again. I held my breath. The screeching sound of "Stukas," the German dive combat airplanes, was deafening. I was in pain. I put my hands on my ears again.

Germans were free to bomb, destroy, and fly anywhere in the city, since the Yugoslavian army surrendered within the first few days of the war.

In March of 1941, Hitler put pressure on Yugoslavia to join the Axis and the Tripartite Pact. The regent of Yugoslavia, under Prince Paul, succumbed to German urging and on March 25[th,] the pact between Germany and Yugoslavia was signed. I remember that day so clearly. We were sitting in a sidewalk café, with Aunt Erna, Uncle Ralph and Aunt Laura, eating *cevapcicy* (elongated hamburgers). A band of gypsies, with their colorful outfits and ribbons, sang and danced while we ate. Their tambourines danced in the air, making a jingling sound. A terrible feeling of death filled the air.

The Serbs, under the leadership of King Peter the 2[nd], who was only 18 yrs old, marched in the streets of Belgrade. They were young and beautiful in their national, royal

uniforms.

Bolje rat nego pakt (Better war than the Tripartite Pact) they recited while marching. My stomach hurt and I got sick. I knew there would be war and we were all going to die.

The screeching of the bombs filled the air, and then one hit. It hit the post office building, eroded six floors down, and then exploded with a force so great that it threw us up in the air and mercilessly dropped us on each other, and then on the floor. Many people were hurt and some were just scared. The basement filled with dust and the smell of explosives. What little light there was went out. The total darkness made it spooky and hard to breathe. We sat there helpless and powerless. All we could do was pray.

I held my hands over my ears. I was hurting, but not as much as before the bomb hit. I removed my hands and realized that the sound had become much louder and sharper. I could even distinguish different sounds and voices. My eardrum, or whatever it was, corrected itself, or snapped back into place from the detonation.

"My ears," I cried out loud.

"I don't want to hear anything about your ears. Just sit down and keep quiet," my mother screamed at me.

I wanted to tell her that the detonation did something to my eardrum and that I could hear. I wanted to share my joy and my miracle with her. But she was too scared and couldn't hear me. She did not want to hear me. I buried my face into my father's chest and cried when I felt my

7

father's comforting hand caress my hair.

My father was a very gentle man. He always had a smile on his face for everyone. My father was the best man in the whole world.

With my newly found capacity to hear in the darkness, I recognized the voices of Uncle Ralph and Aunt Erna. Ralph was my father's brother. He was a baker of French pastries. I also recognized a woman's cries to be that of Aunt Laura. She was my father's sister, and her baby was in her arms.

We all lived in the same neighborhood, so it was not unusual for all of us to end up in the post office building basement. Aunt Laura, was my other mother. Whenever my mother yelled at me, which was frequently, I went to Aunt Laura's house. She was poor. Her husband was an alcoholic and could never make a living.

One time, when I stayed there, my uncle came home drunk. He stank of liquor and sweat. He was absolutely disgusting. He came toward me with his white sleeveless tee shirt, which was yellow with sweat, and tried to kiss me and fondle me. I kept pushing and pushing him away without making a sound. He held me for a few minutes, but since his balance was off, I was able to slip to the floor and crawl away. I never told anyone about this incident because I didn't want my parents to forbid me from going to Aunt Laura's house.

However, I always left after he got home, whether he was drunk or not.

Aunt Laura took in sewing for her survival. She showed me how to thread a needle. She was so good to me, and I loved her very much. She took me to the hospital many times to have my ears and my throat checked. My father helped her out financially many times, which made my mother angry.

We stayed in the basement of the post office for about 24 hours. We had no food, no water or shower, or change of clothes. Inertia had set in, and we couldn't move. By now our eyes had gotten used to darkness, and we were able to see a little. I had to use the bathroom. My mother told me to hold it. My father, without saying a word, got up, took me by the hand, and we made our way between bodies and started looking for a bathroom. We found it. There was some feeble light that came in through a chute from outside. I could see that there was shit everywhere on the seat, all over the floor, even on the walls. The bombs had exploded the water pipes, and the flow of water ceased. I leaned over and threw up on the floor. We burrowed our way back to where my mother was sitting. I stood there looking at her.

"Mom, please help me!" My insides were screaming. She looked away from me, and I felt the warm liquid slide down my legs.

"We have to get out of here! I can't take it any more!" my mother cried.

The Germans bombed Belgrade for seven days and seven nights, with short reprieves between the raids. They were punishing the Serbs for rebelling.

"Where can we go?" my father asked. "The whole city is in ruins and burning." They threw out some names and places, but none seemed safe or worth going to.

"Peter, the milkman," my father exclaimed. "We'll go to Peter's farm. He'll take us in. I know he will."

Before my father moved uptown with his new business, he had a small, neighborhood grocery store. I remember clearly the worn hardwood floors lined with burlap sacks full of rice, beans, garlic and many other groceries. There were shelves and many, many little drawers. Those drawers contained spices that made me sneeze. One day, Peter, the milkman, came to my father's store and said that he needed food for his family and his animals but had no money. My father took a few sheets of newspaper, made a cone out of one, and handed it all to Peter. There were no paper bags, so the newspaper served a double purpose.

"Take what you need," my father said to Peter, smiling. "Don't worry, we'll settle it later."

Our milkman brought us fresh milk every morning and poured it from his large container into ours, which the maid left outside our door the previous evening. We did not have a refrigerator, but we did have an icebox. It was white porcelain and had four feet. Inside, there was a compartment for ice and an area for food. The ice was delivered every other day.

My father heeded his wife's cries, and in between the raids, he gathered our whole family and led us outside of the shelter where our little band of eight ran for our lives.

We headed in the direction of the village where Peter lived, but it was way too far to walk. There were no cars or taxis. Horse and buggy were our only possibility. The city was in chaos. People were running in all directions, and the air was full of dust and flying papers. Some buggies passed us, but they were full of passengers, trying to get out of the city. We approached many, but none wanted to stop because they were full. My father stepped into the middle of the street and grabbed the first horse and buggy that came towards him. The driver of the cart swore at my father, and told him to get the hell out of his way. Without a word, my father reached for my mother's hand, pulled off her 3 carat diamond ring and flashed it to the driver of the carriage. The diamond reflected the brilliance of the sunlight. The driver motioned to all of us to get in the cart, which was lined with straw, as he grabbed the ring from my father's hand. The ride was long and tedious. But as soon as we reached the outskirts of the city, we felt safe from bombs.

Farm Revisited

Chapter 2

FARM REVISITED

The horse and buggy reached the village. The ride was long and dangerous, but we made it. The driver told us to get off in the middle of a field. It felt good to breath the air without smoke and be away from smelly bodies covered with blood. There was still some snow on the ground, and the April air was chilly. We walked through fields of slush and ice. Before we knew it, our little band of frightened souls was standing in front of our milkman's house. We were still wearing the same clothes we were wearing when the bombing began. We brought nothing. We had nothing.

Peter's little farm house had been whitewashed once, but now it looked dirty, with black patches of dirt that adhered to it, and the gray fingers of smoke which ran down its walls.

I remembered having been there before during a happy occasion. There was a wedding. It was exciting and beautiful. The women wore full, colorful skirts and hand embroidered blouses of many colors. They wore multicolored ribbons in their hair. The men wore loose,

white linen pants with hand embroidered tops. On their feet they wore *opanke,* hand made, Turkish leather slippers. I was amazed at how fast their feet moved as they danced the Serbian Kolo to the music of the three men who were playing guitar, tamburica and gusle. (Serbian musical instruments).

But what I remember the best was the pig on the spit. Many people took turns turning the wheel of the spit, where the pig lay in repose. The aroma made my mouth water as the glazed skin of the pig glistened with magnificence. I couldn't wait to bite into it. And then I looked at my mother. She seemed to argue about something with my dad. She was raised very religious, and eating kosher was a big part of her lifestyle. So the sight of the pork made her nauseous.

"You are not going to eat the pig!" she uttered, in horror.

"Don't worry about it, honey. It will all work out." My dad tried to calm her down.

"But you are not going to eat the pig!" she repeated.

"How many times do I have to remind you, sweetheart, that sin does not go into the mouth, it comes out." he laughed, with the delightful prospect of biting into the pig.

I sure loved my dad. He always made the best of any situation and usually came out on top. His family came from a small town in Bosnia, called Brchko. The town was mostly Muslim. Most of the men wore *shalvar,* which were very loose pants made from home spun cotton. They

were almost like a skirt, lose on top and tight on the ankle. Most of the women wore veils over their faces, so that one could only see their eyes. It was a remnant of the Ottoman Empire which ruled that part of Yugoslavia up to the end of the 1st World War. The small town embraced all its occupants equally. They all got along, and that is when my father learned tolerance and love for all people.

My father's family was poor, like most Sephardic Jews in the area. They had lost all their wealth in Spain, after leaving in 1492, due to the Inquisition. They became peddlers and businessmen, ready to pick up and leave any location at any given moment. They all worked for themselves and considered themselves lucky to have comfortable lives and freedom to practice their own religion. With the Spanish Inquisition, came the end of the Golden Age in Spain.

It was Turkey that opened her doors to many Jews from Spain during the Inquisition. The Turkish Sultan, Beyazid, issued a formal invitation to Jews who were expelled from Spain and Portugal. He was also quoted as saying "Ye call Ferdinand a wise king, he who makes his land poor and ours rich." The Jews involved themselves in commerce, and the Turkish economy started to blossom.

During the Golden Age in Spain, the Jews were mostly doctors, philosophers, mathematicians, and advisers to the Muslim Spain. They gave birth to Spinoza, Maimonides, Nahmanides, etc. After all, they were the Grandees.

Some Sephardis were religious, and some were not, but they all spoke Ladino, which was the 14th and 15th

Century Spanish language. It was mixed with Hebrew and other languages where Sephardic Jews lived. But the further they removed themselves from Spain, the more the language diverged from the original Castilian Spanish.

The religious ones read their Torahs regularly. My father lived by the love of God and was always concerned for and cared about other people. He gave food from his grocery store to the needy, like the milkman, even though he knew he would never get paid for it. *Be a good person*, was my father's religion.

Now we were standing in front of Peter's house, again. We were all scared and hungry. There was no food or a place to hide.

My father stood tall and brave as he knocked on Peter's door. An old man wearing a black Greek cap opened the door. He squinted and looked closer at my dad. Then he looked at the eight of us, and then at my father again from a closer proximity. I was scared and cold. I was shaking so hard, that I thought my teeth were going to crack. And I had to go to the bathroom. *Please let us in*, I prayed silently.

The man, who appeared old was wearing drab clothing. He squinted again, stood up on his toes, and threw his arms around my father's neck.

"Sima, Sima Danon! Come in! Come in!" he exclaimed, as he opened the door wide, and motioned with his hand for us to enter.

The circumstances were different from my first visit, but the floors were still only dirt. The furniture was scanty and worn. He called to his wife and whispered something to her. She moved out of the way as he led us to a little bedroom. We entered the room and just stood there looking at each other.

"Isn't this great?" My father broke the silence. But the expression on his face did not match his words. I just wanted to pee. I thought I was going to lose it. I asked for the bathroom. But there was no bathroom in the house.

"I have to pee!" I started to cry. It seemed that no one was concerned about my physical condition. But what was even worse was that they did not want me to be seen or heard. That was the first time in my young years that I took control over my own life and the situation. I ran out of the house and into the bushes. I watched with delight and victory the yellow pee roll over the white snow. "I can take care of myself!" I thought with joy.

When I returned to the room, I found that Peter had brought a whole bunch of straw, spread it all over the small room, and laid some scratchy, home spun wool blankets on top of it. We were crowded, but we were alive and out of the cold, at least for now.

I saw Uncle Ralph and Aunt Erna curled up in one corner, holding on to each other. They looked somewhat like Laurel and Hardy, or the Thin one and the Fat one as we called them in Yugoslavia. Ralph was slight and very thin. He was flexible, like a man made of rubber, and always full of the devil. Erna, on the other hand, was taller and much heavier. I was always amazed at how big her

breasts looked. She had a round face with a milk white complexion, framed by a rich cluster of shiny black hair. They both had a great sense of humor, which at this time was replaced by a grim expression of pain and fright. Their pain due to their lack of children was alleviated by a beautiful German Shepard called Lucy, who was left in the basement of the house during the bombing.

"My poor Lucy," Erna cried at times. "She is probably dead and buried, somewhere under the rubble."

On another small blanket, sat my Aunt Laura trying to nurse my 6 month old cousin. Her milk supply was almost nil because of lack of nourishment and fear. My beloved Aunt Laura was in her 30's, and this was her first child. Her husband was a traveling salesman and did not spend much time at home. But since he had been called into the Yugoslavian army, he had not been heard from. She did not miss him very much. She was much nicer to me than my mom. She always had time to listen to me, and she talked to me like she would talk to an adult. Even after her own baby was born, she never stopped loving me. Her light brown curly hair fell over her face as she bent down caressing and kissing her baby.

One time, the creditors came to her house and wanted to take all her furniture away. And of course, my dad went there with the money and saved her. I am sure that she was much happier being with us than with her worthless, alcoholic husband.

Then, there was my mother. She spread her cashmere coat on the rough blanket, as she sat there trying not to touch the "dirty" straw. Ike was holding on to her so tight, like

a little chimp, that he blended in with her as one. She petted his head, and with her body warmth comforted him into sleep. Even there on the straw she looked beautiful and delicate. She was only 31 years old.

She had seven sisters and two brothers. My mother's family was very wealthy. They owned many properties in their little town of Nish, including the bank. I remember visiting them and swimming in the river, Nishava, which flowed one block from my grandparents' house. When the Nazis came into their town, our family took all the jewelry, opened a door frame, threw the jewelry into the frame, then replaced the planks as if it had never been opened.

All my mother's sisters were married in order of their age. My mother's younger sister liked a local boy and wanted to get married, but couldn't until my mother got married first. Rachel, my mother, was gorgeous, and only seventeen when the marriage broker came to her parents' house and offered my father as a very handsome, successful merchant, who was ten years older than she. My mother did not want to marry him. She wanted a wealthy, sophisticated, religious man, but time did not afford her the luxury of choice. She married a man she did not love, because she felt she had no choice or a voice to express her opinion or her need. They married my mother off at eighteen, and at nineteen she delivered a baby girl, me.

The author's parents. Her mother is holding her.

Consequently, in this little room, even with me and her husband, and only his relatives, she felt totally alone, except for her son.

The dark of the night descended rapidly upon the village, and we still hadn't eaten since the previous day. We could not light the wood stove to cook something, or even put on the light. This would have been an invitation and an attraction for the German bombers. Peter brought in a small candle and covered the windows with a black sheet.

"You must be hungry," Peter's wife said as she walked into the room, holding a few small cans without labels and a can opener. She also had some bread wrapped in a beautiful hand embroidered towel.

My father took the cans, opened them, and smelled the

contents.

"Smells good. What is it?" he asked looking at Marica, Peter's wife.

"It is good. Soldiers gave to us," she responded with pride.

From the looks and the smell of the contents, my father thought it was French Pate. " I am sure it is delicious, but what is it?" my father asked again, looking at Marica.

Everyone was very hungry and eager to satisfy their natural urges. Marica hesitated for a moment, then said softly, "It is meat of horse."

My father swallowed hard and almost choked on his own saliva. My mother put her hand on her mouth, while others looked in horror.

"I am hungry," my brother Ike cried for the first time, aroused by the scent of food.

Without saying a word, my father tore pieces of bread, smeared them with horse meat, and started doling them out. For a few moments no one moved. The hesitation was on all their faces. Then suddenly, all the hands went up in sweet resignation.

For the next few days we survived on rations of corn, shares of bread, horse meat, and water from the well. There was very little milk, which was divided between me, my brother Ike, and my baby cousin.

I remember going into the barn, tugging on the cow's udder and pointing it into my mouth. The milk was warm and sweet and wet all over my face. I loved it. There in the barn, with the smell of the cow and comfort of the warm milk, I forgot the anguish of the situation.

The Nazis did not waste their ammunition on unimportant Yugoslavian peasants, so we were spared from the bombs in the village.

At night, we stood outside the little house, in the dark, crying and praying, as we watched our beloved city burn. I held on to my dad, crying and asking, "Why doesn't God send some rain and put out that horrible fire?" I couldn't breathe. By this time, the air was thick with smoke and soot as the flames danced all around us like a ring of fire.

The emotional pain was unbearable, but the fear was even greater. "What will happen to us?" We knew what was happening to the Jews in Poland and Russia. And we were also aware about the "Crystal Night." I didn't know what that was until my father explained to me that on November 9th and 10th of 1938, Nazi Gangs all over Germany, broke Jewish store windows, pilfered merchandise, and wrote "Pig Jews" and drew the stars of David all over the walls. They also destroyed Jewish synagogues and then set them on fire. Many German people were shocked with this event. Most of the German Jews blended in with the Germans. They were considered Germans first, and then Jews.

"Where can we go? Where can we hide?" was our predominant concern.

Two days later, my father got restless being cooped up in Peter's house, so he went into Belgrade to check on his store and the general situation of the city.

After he sold the grocery store, at my mother's insistence, he opened an elegant leather goods salon in the center of Belgrade. The store was beautiful, and he carried very fine leather gloves, bags, belts, purses, and small traveling cases. In the back of the store my father started a small factory which produced the goods he sold. Every item was handmade to perfection. All of his machinery and all his luscious leather, which lay in large rolls against the factory wall, were all purchased from Germany.

My great joy used to be when my father came home for lunch, as they all did in Yugoslavia, he would bring me a bag full of little pieces of leather. I cut the pieces and sewed them together, creating my own purse designs. My father said that very soon, I would be his best designer. I loved sitting in my father's lap and eating my lunch, which made my mother angry.

"You are too big to sit on your father's lap," she would complain. "Here, sit in your own chair." But her words fell on our deaf ears.

A few days went by, and we didn't know what was going on with my father. There was no way he could reach us or inform us of what was happening. When he finally returned from the city, my father was wearing a heavy, large black coat and a large hat. The hat came way down over his face, hiding it. Peter, followed by the rest of us, walked outside to welcome him back. My dad was

heavy, with a bulge on one side, and his steps were accelerated as he approached us. Before we could say anything, my dad unbuttoned his coat, revealing a huge ring of Swiss cheese. He lifted his head and looked at us with a great, mischievous smile.

"Look what I've got. Just look. Isn't it magnificent?" he said with joy. "I stole it. I just went into a store, took it and walked out. Can you believe? I stole the cheese, and I stole this coat too."

Nobody seemed interested in my father's adventure. They wanted to know what was going on in the city.

"What happened with the store? Is the building still standing? What about all the equipment?" my mother lamented.

"Gone. All gone. The equipment, the leather, the inventory, all gone." my father responded, with tears in his eyes.

As we all gorged on the delicious treat, my father brought us up to date on the situation in the city.

"It is very grim. Nazis everywhere. Buildings destroyed. The smell of death fills the city." He wiped his face and rubbed his eyes.

"Workers are pulling bodies from the ruins. And.... and..... there were already a few cases of typhoid." His words came out with great difficulty. "There is no water or food, except what the German trucks dole out."

"And the Jews? What is happening with the Jews?" my uncle asked.

"What do you think is happening with the Jews?" my father snapped. "Those bastards already started. There were only a few Jews on the streets cleaning the rubble, and they all wore the yellow armbands with the Star of David. Other Jews are afraid to go out on the street for fear of being picked up and shot on the spot. That's what's happening to the Jews."

I knew that there was a reason to be scared, but not in my wildest dreams could I conceive of the inhumanity and torture that awaited us.

The bombing stopped, and we went back to the city and our house, which was still standing with a lot of fallen plaster and cracked walls without windows.

The Marching Boots

Chapter 3

THE MARCHING BOOTS

The Nazis marched into Belgrade and the nightmare began. There was no one throwing flowers at the invaders. Serbs hated Nazis as much as did the Jews, while the Croatians put on the SS uniforms and shared the glory of the dark victory.

After we left the village, in spite of all the dust and fallen plaster at our house, we were relieved to find that it had not been vandalized and that nothing was taken. We rolled up our sleeves and started to clean, but since there was no water, all we could do was dust.

I looked at the dirty kitchen with broken tiles and broken windows. I remembered the way it looked before the war.

It was warm, and it always smelled good, with freshly made bread. One day my mother made a round loaf of bread, baked it and left it on the stove to cool off. I was left home with the babysitter, since the maid had a day off, and that bread sure smelled good. So we each tore off a piece of bread, put a lot of butter on it, and ate it. And

then we took another piece. And then another, until the whole loaf was gone. When my parents came home, they laughed and patted my stomach.

The shiny living room hardwood floors were adorned with Persian rugs. In the kitchen, the cast iron stove had a lot of chrome, which the maid spent hours polishing. I especially remember Friday evenings, or Shabat. The house was spotless. The candles were burning on the kitchen table, throwing off a soft light and reflecting on the floor to ceiling ceramic tiles. The aroma of food penetrated every pore in my body. The best thing, however, was the bath. The water was heated on the stove and poured into the tub.

My brother and I would get the first bath, where we frolicked with the soap suds. The second bath with more hot water added, was reserved for my dad, and then my mother. The maid was the last one to bathe, and then the soapy water was used to wash the floor. My father would take each of us children out of the tub, wrap us into a towel and take us to the kitchen where my mother and the maid were waiting to spill their love on us.

And now the kitchen was cold and smelled of death. There was no drinking water, so the Nazis went through town with a water wagon and doled it out. The Jews marked by the yellow armbands were not allowed to get in line for water.

There was still some old, stale water in the toilet tank, which we boiled to kill the typhus and other germs. The taste was bad. It was worse than drinking some horrible medicine.

At 11 yrs old, I was fearless, especially since my father taught me that I could do anything I set my mind to. I looked into my father's eyes and declared, "I am going down to the water wagon to get some water."

"No way, sweetheart, I would rather die of thirst than let you go down there!" my father exclaimed.

I took the glass pitcher, and when no one was looking, I sneaked out the door, down the stairs and to the street, where I got in line for water. At first I was excited, because I disobeyed my father, which I had not done often, but then the fear showed up.

The Nazis were mean. They pushed people around, and when they marched, you could hear the sound of their boots echo on the cobble stone streets for many blocks away. I stood in line with other people. I waited. I started to shake. I looked around. My knees were knocking at each other and my whole body shook like I was put in a freezer. It was very hard to hold on to the glass pitcher. As I approached the wagon, I held it with both my hands and held my breath. I was afraid to look up at the Nazi, so all I could see were the black, shiny boots which frightened me so.

I extended my little hands carefully, not to waste a drop, and watched the clear, life-giving liquid climb onto itself, trying to reach the top of my pitcher. Without waiting for it to fill up, I pulled the pitcher and was ready to run, when the Nazi grabbed my arm so tightly that I think he stopped the circulation. I wanted to scream, but, I was so scared that when I opened my mouth, no sound came out. He started to shake my arm trying to get a glimpse of my

face. My dark brown, curly hair and big dark eyes were my dead giveaway. I was a typical Sephardic, Jewish little girl.

With his other hand he reached for the pitcher, yanking it out of my hands, screaming, "You pig Jew. You Pig. Did you think you could get away with this? Judenschwein!"

And while still screaming at me, he let the glass pitcher drop on the cobble stone street, spilling the lifeline that water afforded us.

For one second, I watched the priceless, clear water run down the street and embrace each stone, as it skipped over it. I tried to free my arm from the Nazi's grip, while only looking at his boots. And when he relaxed his grip for a second, I ran to our house, crying hysterically while the Nazi continued to dole out water and grumble against the Jews.

When I got in the house my mother screamed at me, as usual, for disobeying, while I just held onto my daddy's arm and cried hysterically.

During the next few weeks, more and more Nazis filled our city. The streets were lined with tanks and army trucks and soldiers who walked and marched down every street.

Because we lived in a Christian area, the Nazis had not discovered our house yet, so many of our friends would congregate with us. They would sneak in at night under the cover of darkness and spend the night. They slept on couches and floors. I couldn't understand why all those

people did not go to their own houses. What I really wanted to know was, *"Who was Bertha?"* I never saw her before. She even talked funny, like she was from another country. She did not talk much, but nobody wanted to tell me who she was. At times I thought that not even my parents knew where she came from. All I was told was that their houses were destroyed by bombs and people had no place to go, so we let them in. We were just grateful that the Nazis did not raid our house, yet.

My Aunt Laura never heard from my uncle, so she decided that he was already dead. Her little baby, Danica, was really cute. She was a plump little doll, with rosy cheeks, and curly shiny light brown hair. I wanted to play with her and hold her, but my aunt constantly reminded me that she was not a toy. She was growing up fast, and she would never know her father. They stayed with us, because Aunt Laura was afraid to go home. I did not mind that at all.

There wasn't much food, but we still had the sacks of potatoes, onions, rice, beans and dried bell peppers which were strung on a rope, and allowed to dry. Since we did not have an electric refrigerator, we had to rely on foods that would last a long time, stored in the cellar. There were also garlands of garlic, hanging on the balcony facing the garden. I loved eating homemade hot bread dipped in heavy olive oil and chunks of raw garlic.

Everybody was eating garlic, because they said that garlic would prevent us from getting typhoid and other diseases. It also made everybody stink. I hated it when they came close to me, pinched my cheeks and breathed that awful smell into my face.

There were other relatives who came to our house, ate and left. And sometimes, they sat and played cards without talking. No voices ever came from our house. The absence of sound was painful. My parents didn't want any noise to come from the house, so as not to attract attention. Occasionally my baby cousin cried, but was shushed immediately, or Ike asked for something loudly. He, too, was kept quiet with his toys while I tried to make sense of that crazy situation. I always asked questions, which drove my mother crazy. She had no patience for me. She did not have much patience for me even before the war, but now I became just an irritant to her.

She frequently reminded me not to drip food on my dress. I hated the dresses she gave me. They had been made by the same seamstress that made my mother's dresses from the French Mode Magazines. I wasn't allowed to play or get dirty. I hated that. And I had to take my dress off as soon as I got in the house, and put on some play clothes.

After we left the milkman's village, Uncle Ralph and Aunt Erna went home and were terribly happy to find out that Lucy, the German Shepard, was not only alive, but that she had 3 puppies, which looked like little balls of fur.

I often walked a few blocks to their house to see the darling little puppies. My uncle's Bakery was totally destroyed. What the vandals left, the Nazis took. The Croatian Ustashe, dressed in Nazi uniforms and black boots, targeted all the Jewish businesses and homes. They knew who lived where, and who had money. They were worse to us than the Nazis. They were like vultures,

devouring their prey before the body was even cold.

Croatian Ustashe created the third largest concentration and extermination camp in the world during WW ll. It was erected in 1941 near Zagreb, Croatia and dismantled in April 1945. This was the infamous JASENOVAC. The Ustashe leader was Dr. Ante Pavelich. They were responsible for the deaths of six hundred thousand Jews, Serbs and Gypsies. Those victims were collected from Zagreb, Sarajevo and all small towns in Croatia. They only kept alive those men whose talents they could use, such as pharmacists, doctors, engineers and such. Thousands of Jewish children were burned alive by the Ustashe. But the most brutal was a former priest, Miroslav Filipovic-Majstorovic, who personally killed thousands of prisoners with his own hands. One time they even had a contest as to who could kill the most prisoners in one hour. One barbaric Ustasha prided himself that he cut the throats of thousands of Jews, so he won a bottle of wine and a roast pig.

Croatian Ustashe were so barbaric and so brutal that they would take Jewish children and take out their eyes, just for pleasure.

*

One day when I went to see Lucy and the puppies, I heard pleading screams coming out of the my aunt's house. I was too scared to go in, so I hid outside in the bushes and listened. I heard my aunt pleading in German, "Please don't. Please let her be. Please. Please don't." And then gun shots, followed by my aunt's screams and then silence. I crouched even lower, not making a sound, hardly even breathing. I thought that my aunt and uncle had both been murdered.

A while later, I heard the sound of the black marching boots on the steps as they were leaving my uncle's house. There was not a sound coming from inside. I waited a few more minutes and ran in. There in the basket, Lucy lay in a pool of blood and the three little fur balls were not gray anymore. They were red, soaked in their own blood. My aunt lay on the floor, motionless, next to the basket and all her dead "children." Those dogs were her children. The Nazis heard the dogs bark, went into the house and shot them.

I thought that my aunt was also dead. But she had just fainted, and my uncle was kneeling next to her, gently kissing her eyes and forehead.

Before the war, I used to go to their house and I always wanted to help with making cookies. My uncle would let me, under the condition that I whistle all the time. I was very happy, until I realized that if I whistled, I could not indulge in the delicious cookies. He was very clever, my uncle. In the evening we would all get in one bed, and my Aunt Erna would peel apples and pears, then feed me and my uncle, Ralph. When we finished eating the fruit, she would lead us into a song. And at times even Lucy,

the German Shepard would join in with her soulful wail.

As soon as my aunt came to, they took a few pieces of clothing, grabbed me by the hand, and we all crawled against the facades of the houses, trying to blend in, as we went to our house. They left everything they owned in the world behind. They left their love and hearts there, in that bloody basket, where their pets lay lifeless.

One day, the Germans announced that all men had to come out of their houses and clean out the bodies which were starting to rot, and smell, under the rubble left from the bombing.

My mother pleaded with my dad not to go, but he felt it was his civic duty to help with the clean up. Each night he came home, he brought another horror story. He told us about the body parts he pulled out, and the time he saw an arm, thinking it was a person, but as he reached for it, he found himself shaking hands with a lifeless arm. He smelled bad when he came home. He was covered with white powdery dust and his hands were dirty and bleeding. The Nazis had not yet started picking up Jews because they needed them to clean up the city.

One day my father left the house as usual. We waited for his return. We waited, and waited and waited. The night came. We still waited. The night passed and my daddy wasn't home yet. We all knew that he was taken by the Nazis and placed in a holding cell. The men in the holding cells were hostages, and if one German soldier got killed during that week, the Nazis would take 100 Jews from the holding cell, line them up on the street and shoot them. The bodies were always left on the street for

many days, as a warning to others.

I never prayed so hard in my life. I prayed that no Nazi would be shot that week.

Every night, I stood at the window, looking at the ghost-like city below and cried. I missed my daddy. I was so afraid for him. I was so afraid that those horrible Nazis would kill my daddy.

And what would I do then? What would I do without my dad? Who would take care of us? Who would take care of me? At night, I would put on my daddy's pajamas, dragging the leggings behind me while I kept tripping every step of the way. His pajama top had the most beautiful mother of pearl buttons. I pretended that those buttons were magic. So I stood at the window, and looked up in the sky, rubbing the buttons. I cried all night, rubbing the magic buttons and wished my daddy was back, alive.

In the holding cell, the men just sat on the floor and waited and prayed. Occasionally, a soldier would come in bringing in some colored water, which was supposed to be soup, and pour it into a tin cup for each man. Once they were given some bread crumbs. They just sat there waiting for death to come and claim its own. Each man hoping it would not be him.

A week passed and no Nazi got killed. My father was released from the holding cell. He looked like a ghost. No shave. Same clothes. No shower. But alive. It was only a small victory, but for me it was my whole world.

By this time the plumbing was restored and we could flush the toilets, but the water was still not safe for drinking. We had to boil it in order to kill all the bacteria and germs.

After my father came home from the holding cell, he and other men would sit in our kitchen, in a cloud of smoke from cigarettes, listening to the radio. Some strange people would come to the house, dressed really weird, with black scarfs, long black coats, whispering and then leaving just as mysteriously as they came.

My mother told me I was too young to understand everything, and I should not be asking all those questions. My mother sneaked out of the house every once in a while to sell some of her jewelry and buy food.

Someone had brought some "Biscochos," a Sephardic cookie, and someone else brought Turkish coffee beans. They ground it in our kitchen, and cooked it in a Turkish pot, called "Djezva." It was a small pot made of copper with a long handle which they held over the fire of the wood stove. The smell of coffee was wonderful, but the coffee was very strong and bitter. They would put a small cube of sugar in their mouth, then take a sip of that strong, bitter Turkish coffee. There was always someone who would turn the coffee cup upside down, watch the grounds spread in all directions and then read that person's fortune. They sure were weird.

"How long do you think this war will last?" a heavy man with glasses asked.

"Not very long, I hope."

"I hope you are right. But I don't believe it," someone volunteered. "Look what they are doing to all of Europe"

"I wonder how long before Russia falls?" another voice observed.

I don't ever remember meeting some of those people. I guess they were my father's business associates. Anyway, I stood there in the kitchen, quiet and invisible. I couldn't figure it out. *Was I really invisible, or did they just not see me?* Sometimes, I would play a game with myself. I would hide, or just stand in the middle of a room and see if anyone would see me. And at times I would look at my tiny fingers, or hands, and wonder if others could see my hands, also.

"Russia isn't going to fall. Remember what happened to Napoleon?" I said to all the deaf ears. I wanted to show them that I knew who Napoleon was and what happened to him. I knew that as he approached Moscow, the Russians burned everything in sight, and Napoleon and his army either starved, or froze to death. That was the lesson in my history class.

One year before the war, I started going to a new, all girl gymnasium school. It was so beautiful that we had special shoes we changed into when we entered the school, so as not to scratch the floors. I liked going to school. I studied German, French, History, Math, and many other subjects. I always had a problem with the calligraphy because I was too impatient to take time for thin and fat lines.

Our teachers were very strict. As soon as we entered our

home room, we had to take our seats and sit tall and straight, cross our hands across our chest, and be very quiet. Talking was not allowed. We had to have a notebook and a pencil on the desk. I still remember well the smell of the new wooden desk. I would close my eyes and pretend that I was out on a farm or in a forest. If we broke any of the rules, the teacher would call us to the front of the class and hit our extended palms with the ruler. I got hit one time, because I pushed a girl who told me that she hated me because I killed Jesus Christ. That day I went home crying, because I got spanked by the teacher, and I told my father that I didn't kill anybody. "I swear, Daddy. I did not kill anybody." Obviously, Jesus and Christianity were not my subjects.

Shortly after I entered my beautiful school, a pact was signed between Yugoslavia and Germany, and I, with all other Jewish kids, were thrown out of our beautiful public schools. We had to enroll in private schools with all the derelicts who were not allowed in public schools. What stayed in my mind mostly from that school was that the kids were bigger and older than I was. Many of them were repeating the same classes and were not so bright. They, also, were not so well behaved as were the young people in my public school. In the hallway there was a water dispenser. It was an aluminum tub with many tap faucets coming from the wall. It looked like pigs' tits, where the young ones came to nurse. Next to it, on a chain, hung a dented, aluminum cup. It looked like the cup of a blind man begging for alms. This cup was used by all the kids to drink water. I always got sores on my lips, which I got from the cup.

When my mother realized what was happening, she

forbade me to drink from that cup, and packed another cup in my lunch bag. But, then other kids wanted to use my cup and took it away from me.

When I entered that school, I had very rich, glorious shiny brown hair. But when I got infested with hundreds of lice, my mother took a pair of shears, and cut it off. I kicked and screamed as I watched my gorgeous curls cover the kitchen floor. She then took a white towel, put it on her lap and I lay my head on it. Then she took gasoline, put it in a cup, and with a piece of cotton rubbed it into my hair. A few minutes later, we would watch and count all the dead lice that fell on the white towel. And those that were still alive, my mother would put between her two thumb nails and smash them. I loved to hear them pop.

One evening, in June of 1941, the men in our kitchen were still speculating about the end and duration of the war. Suddenly the news came on the radio and everyone stopped taking. The Belgrade Station, which was controlled by the Germans, came in clear, but the voice from England was muffled and almost muted. They huddled closer, with their ears practically on top of the radio.

"Doesn't look good," were the only sounds coming from the select group.

"Doesn't look good at all," someone whispered between cigarette puffs.

"What are we going to do?"

"Where will we go?"

"They are shipping all the Jews from Germany to Poland for hard labor."

"Why do they do that?" a woman asked.

"I heard that they have a camp there where they put all the Jews before killing them. They take out all the Jewish gold teeth and dentures and salvage them."

Auschwitz and Treblinka were not known to us at that time. No one knew of the experiments the Nazis did on live human beings in those camps. No one knew about all the women and children who were taken to a large shower room and were told to undress completely for the shower. Young girls were so painfully ashamed to bare their bodies and stand naked for all to see. No, they were not told the truth and those were not showers. It was gas that penetrated their nostrils and their skin and opened the door for death, which solved the Jewish problem for Nazis.

"I heard that they are going to take all the Jews from Yugoslavia and ship them to Germany."

" I bet you, we'll never see Germany. They'll shoot us as soon as they get us out of the Logor (Concentration Camp).

"I think the war will be over before you know it, now that Russia got involved."

"You don't know what you are talking about. The only

41

way to survive is to go to America."

"Yeah, sure. They'll send a boat just for you."

"I wonder if there is a way for us to go to Palestine?" another man said.

"Even if you got there, you couldn't get in. Those British bastards are guarding the ports with their lives."

I didn't know much about Palestine, except that I remembered while still in Yugoslavia, going to a Hebrew school for Hanukah and getting a small linen bag full of oranges, dates and peanuts, all from Palestine. I also remember that after all the prayers, we would all repeat, "Next year, in Jerushalaim." (Jerusalem)

Around 1940, Churchill, the Prime Minister of England, didn't want to antagonize the Arabs, so the British did not allow any Jews to enter Palestine, which was under British mandate. Even though this was the time when Jews needed a place the most, in order to survive, they were barred from getting in. In fact, many Jews who made their trek to Palestine, were refused entry into Palestine, and were shipped off to the Island of Cyprus. There they were placed in a camp with hardly any food or water, and no sanitation. Many Jews died of dysentery and other diseases. Some were even sent back to their countries of origin, which most did not survive.

Unfortunately, Zionism, which was started by Theodor Herzl, who was a writer in Paris in 1895, was not strong or influential enough to save any Jews or even influence

any one country to save them.

I listened to the people in our kitchen talk. Men and women, desperate, wanting to survive, but sentenced to death without a cause, without a trial, without a reason. Their only sin was being born Jewish. They loved their families and wanted to live in peace, and watch their grandchildren grow up, yet, they all looked into the face of death.

When they talked, it sounded like they were fighting. I was scared. They were scared. Nobody knew what was going to happen to us, but we all knew it would be terrible. The thought of America sounded good, but at that time, it was only a dream, a fantasy which would never materialize.

Death Camp At Gajmishle

Chapter 4

DEATH CAMP AT SAJMISHTE

In the beginning of November 1941, my father was picked up by the Nazis and taken into a concentration camp.

We did not hear from him, or know if he was dead or alive, for months. I slept in my father's pajamas as I did often, looked out the window at the stars and the sky and knew my father was alive, and was coming back to me.

But there was no trace of him, or any other men who were nabbed at that time. My mother and I went to many different official Nazi buildings which were teeming with German soldiers in black leather boots. A few times we were kicked in the legs and backs. It was very painful.

One time, we stopped in front of a building while my mother just stared. She grabbed me by the hand and started pulling me toward this tall, scary Nazi, dressed in all black, wearing a leather coat.

She extended her hand, and called him by his name. He, in fact, was not even German, he was a Croatian Ustasha, dressed like German S.S. Trooper.

He looked at my mother, mumbling "Judenschwein," and took out his gun. He looked at me, then at my mother and

started to shoot. A few shots went around our feet, and a few seemed to fly around our heads. I started to scream, pulling my mother's hand, which seemed to be attached to mine.

"He won't hurt us," she whispered. "He couldn't do that," she repeated, almost calmly.

She remembered Sveta when he was a young man, and used to come to my father's leather good store. He had just graduated from what was the equivalent of high school and had started to sell sewing machines, which were made in Germany. My father was debating about a piece of equipment, but bought it, just to help him get started. My father also lent him money when he was short. He was such a lovely young man. Very polite and genteel. Every time he came to our store, he kissed my mother's hand and told her how beautiful she was and that he would never forget her and my dad.

And now, we were standing in front of him and he was shooting at us. As long as I live, I will never know if he, himself, was afraid to acknowledge us as friends, or if he had adopted the current trend of robbing and killing Jews, as all other Ustashes did.

My mother turned around crying and started walking away, when another torrent of bullets spilled around us. Still having a hard time believing, my mom pulled me by the hand, realizing that he was not a friend. I guess the sound of the gun and the bullets whizzing around us showed his real intentions.

After a while, we heard the news. In December of 1941, a concentration death camp was established at Sajmishte, a few miles outside of Belgrade. This facility used to be the

fairgrounds and it had many different barns.

It was located on the River Sava near the entrance to Belgrade. After the Nazis entered Yugoslavia, this area became Croatian territory. At first the Germans were going to take the Jewish men to Germany, but then they reconsidered and asked the Croatian Ustashe to use Sajmishte as a concentration camp. The *Logor*, death camp, was meant for Serbian resistance fighters, Serbian Jews and subsequently the Romas (Gypsies).

After the Nazis exterminated all the Jewish men, they, under the command of SS trouper Harold Turner, collected about 10,000 Jewish women and children. They were put in the camp and then they were told that they were being taken to German labor camps. But, of course, that was never the intention. They were gassed in the trucks, supposedly, on the way to Germany. In total, about 66,000 Jews from Yugoslavia were exterminated.

Gypsies, who originally came from India, were disbursed all over Europe. The Nazis started hunting down Gypsies early in the war, because they said that the Gypsies would genetically pollute the Aryan Race. All in all, between 250,000 and 500,000 Gypsies were exterminated. First, they were made to register, then they were sterilized, and finally they were put into concentration camps where they all perished.

The Nazis also did not have a great love for homosexuals and lesbians, whether they were German or other nationalities. They were disgusted with them, and they too, became a target for extermination.

After we heard of the Camp at Sajmishte, my mother and I went to see if my dad was there, but nobody would talk to us. As I spoke some German, I kept asking all of the German soldiers how we could find out if my dad was there, or where he could be.

But again, all we got was kicked and called pig Jew. We got hit with bayonets and shot at, just as before. Many times we ran away frightened, but returned to ask the same question, over and over again. We were standing near this huge wooden gate with barbed wire on top, when the Nazis opened it to let some civilians in. There seemed to be some confusion and we took advantage of it and cautiously made our way in with the other people. We just persisted and inquired, over and over.

There were German soldiers everywhere. The skies were gray and pregnant with rain. The air was heavy, as the chilled December air enveloped the surroundings. The camp was filled with older Jewish men, or at least they seemed old, as they sat on the damp ground, reading their prayer books. Some had ragged blue and white prayer shawls around their necks, and torn shirts, without jackets or sweaters, shivering. *They must be freezing*, I thought.

Nobody talked to anybody, yet the whole place seemed like a beehive, teeming with activities. My mother and I frantically flew from one person to another, asking if anyone saw or heard of my father. Most people just sped by us without responding. They moved away as fast as they were approached. Finally, a man without looking at us, made a motion with his hand and ran away. Two women, mother and daughter, frightened and hoping, followed his sign and approached the front of a large

barn, with holes in the roof and wet straw on the ground. The stench was horrendous and reminded me of a chicken coop.

We entered the barn holding our breath, while continuing to ask for my father, "Sima Danon." An old man told us to follow him. Here, he pointed to a skeleton like figure, curled up in a fetal position, shivering. He was almost naked, covered with black and blue marks all over. Both of us bent down to look at this creature which looked like a bunch of bones, covered with human membrane.

The face looked up. The eyes were sunken into the skull. The hair was dirty, matted and cropped. The beard was long, filthy, red with some gray in it. The image looked over a hundred years of age. *This couldn't be my dad*, I thought. *My dad is only 41 years old. And, why was he almost naked?*

This skeletal figure started to get up with difficulty. A grimace, resembling a smile, appeared on the skull. I backed off. I was frightened. I could hear my mother's silent screams, as she moved closer to the image of a man, and reached out. He managed to stand up, draping himself over her body. I felt paralyzed. I opened my mouth to speak, but no voice came out. I wasn't even sure that I could, or wanted to touch him. My insides were screaming in confusion, with anger and with pain. I wanted my handsome, loving father back.

I couldn't understand what they did to my dad, and why. My father always helped everyone in need. He was such a good man. *Why did God let this happen?*

I remembered when I took Hebrew classes, that they taught us that God was all powerful and He took care of good people. *Then why didn't God stop them from hurting my daddy? Did God take a nap, while the Nazis did all this? They must have lied to me. There is no God. If there were a God, He could never let the Nazis hurt us like this.*

Yet, the reality was, that this was my father. They had taken a young, handsome, healthy man and turned him into an old skeleton. I watched my mom kiss his sunken eyes, his dirty beard, his smelly body. She took off her coat and swung it over his bare shoulders. They both cried, as they held on to each other and to the precious gift of life, while hoping for a miracle.

I decided that there may be a God after all, because a miracle did occur. German guards could never be bribed, but Croatian Ustashe could. By bribing the guards, we were able to bring my father food and fresh clothing. We even brought enough for him to share with those who had no family to bring them things, or visit them. As soon as my father's strength returned, he started getting involved with the camp activities and helping anyone he could. He was not different in that disgusting, filthy place than he was in peace time.

The Nazis were masters of torture. They knew how to create it, and how to perpetuate it. They created a government from within the camp consisting of Jewish men. There were about 500 men who distributed the scanty food, guarded the fence from inside and administered odd jobs to different prisoners. Each of those men was picked for a specific purpose, and since they all wanted to survive they played up to the Nazis.

Some were even meaner to their brethren then the Nazis themselves.

While in the camp, a man with the Hungarian accent came to my father and introduced himself.

"Mr. Danon. Sam Danon. I was appointed head of this camp, and if there is anything I can do for you, I will."

My dad looked at him in disbelief. *Who was this man? What was his game? Why was he nice?* People in this situation only wanted to survive. *What did he want?* All kinds of questions filled his mind when the man continued. This was what my father related to us later.

"The woman you took into your home, after the bombing, by the name of Bertha..."

My father listened, nodding his head.

"Bertha is my wife. She told me, you and your family took her in, gave her food, and never asked any questions." The man wiped his swollen, teary eyes, with his dirty shirt sleeve, stopped for a minute and then continued.

"We lived in a small town near the Hungarian border. And when the Nazis picked me up and shipped me out here, my wife.... she.... she came to Belgrade to find me and just spend a little more time near me... before...beforewell before they shipped me out again. So if there is anything you want, just ask."

My father thought quickly and asked the man to give him

51

a position of a sanitation supervisor. I guess what that meant, was that he had to clean, and take out the garbage from the German army kitchen, and some army barracks. But it also meant that he had the freedom to move from one section of the camp to another, without being stopped and asked for I. D. each time.

The camp was divided into many sections with tall wooden fences, so one could not see over, or go to any section, except where one were assigned. A lot of men were brought in from other parts of Yugoslavia, so they had no family or visitors at all. We visited my father frequently because we didn't know when the men would be shipped out, or killed. We wanted to spend as much time with him as we possibly could.

In the meantime, the Gestapo were taking hundreds of men, three times a day, every day, on the pretense that they were shipping them off to Germany for hard labor, when in fact they needed more room for other men they collected from all parts of Yugoslavia. Down deep inside, all the Jews knew that they would never reach Germany or any other place. They were made to dig trenches just outside of Belgrade, which were to become their own mass graves.

It was obvious to my dad that he also would be taken away any day, but in the meantime, he tried to help as many people as possible, especially since he was able to move from one section to another.

In the camp, there was an infirmary. The only doctor there, was a young Jewish man who had been kidnapped, and had not seen any of his family since that time. His

mother, the only one who survived, came to the camp, but was unable to get a pass to see him. One day she came and cried and pleaded with my father to arrange some kind of a meeting. My dad whispered to her to cry out and pretend to faint. She did. My father lifted her up and carried her into the infirmary. He was stopped a few times, but he successfully delivered the yearning mother to her son. My dad watched as mother and son held on to each other for the last time.

Later on, after the Nazis started collecting women and children, the infirmary was used by the Nazis for experimentation on Jews. They took a pregnant woman who was ready to deliver her baby, and pushed the baby back inside, just to see how long the baby could stay inside the mother's body before the baby, or the mother, or both, died.

One night, shortly after the men went to sleep, a siren went off, followed by the tormenting sound of the marching black leather boots. The Jews were brought out into the largest court yard for selection. All the men were lined up in a row. The Nazis paraded up and down the line, looking at each man's face, tearing at their nervous systems. The men shivered. They were nervous, frightened and freezing in the dark, damp, December night. Their bodies moved involuntarily. Some appeared to be dovening, (bowing forward in prayer). Torn shirts barely covered their thin, beaten bodies.

A reflector spotlight moved from face to face, in step with the Nazi. He looked at a face and stopped, the reflector illuminated it, blinding the Jew. His cold stare paralyzing every nerve and every muscle in the Jew's

body. Then while still glaring at the first person, the Nazi would grab the person next to the shivering man, yelling "Judenschwein," and the German soldiers would come and drag the second person out.

Later on, my father described to me how his mind filled with fear and anxiety, and what his thoughts were. *Is this it? Is this the end? Am I never to see my family again? Why God? Why? Why? Why is this nightmare happening to your Chosen people? Why have you forsaken me, my God?*

My father's thoughts raged, all the while his body shaking, like a man with Parkinson's disease. *If only I had a sign from YOU that YOU are here. Or, is this not an end, but a new beginning to where there are no labels, no prejudice, only an eternal YOU?*

The torment gnawed at his insides. A man in the line fainted. The Nazi walked toward him with brisk, marching steps. With the end of his bayonet, he poked at the Jew on the ground. The Jew did not move. The head Nazi walked over there also, took out his pistol from his halter, aimed and pulled the trigger, while the rest of the men watched in horror, as the warm, red blood splattered all over the bare almost frozen ground.

The Nazi continued to walk, looking into one frightened face after another. He stopped in front of my father. His face cold and expressionless, only his eyes revealing the hate and terror he spread.

"Whom are they going to choose tonight?" all the Jews wondered as they shivered.

The Nazi smiled an evil smile as he started to point at my father. My father felt the Nazi's eyes, like cold steel piercing his body. His limbs became numb and his mind paralyzed with fear. He knew he was standing on the thin line between life and death.

The Nazi's hand moved towards my father and in my father's mind the hand kept growing and growing until it reached the size of a monster. And as it was about to land on my dad's shoulder, the Nazi grabbed the man next to my dad and threw him on the ground, while yelling all the while, "You pig, Jew. You pig, Jew."

My poor daddy felt as though the blood had been drained out of him. He miraculously remained standing up without fainting. The selecting continued for the next few hours, until one hundred men were picked. Slowly, deliberately engulfed in horror and fear, they were shoved inside the army trucks and driven away. Shortly after they departed, a myriad of shots echoed in the darkness in unison with the cries of the slaughtered men. The remaining Jews, with their broken bodies and minds, were ushered back to their places in the damp, smelly straw.

How much pain can a man endure? And which is greater, physical or mental pain? The body knows how to utilize the self-preserving tools such as fainting, or blacking out, in order to escape the pain. But the mind, what does the mind do? Go insane? Become schizophrenic? Pray for death? Death which is usually feared, is now welcomed. Death. Sweet peaceful Death, which is now more easily accepted than the pain of watching the ones you love being taken away from you and slaughtered like animals.

The quiet returned to the night. My dad lay on the damp straw and peered through the cracks of the dilapidated, old wooden walls and roof of the barn. Outside, the night was cold and dark, like his hope for survival. As he started to resign to his spent body, he noticed that the clouds had parted revealing the most glorious star, shining so brightly that it seemed to call to him. My father sat up invigorated with the magical energy of the universe.

"Is this my sign? What does it mean? How? Oh my God, you did not forsake me after all." The tears rushed down his face. He knew. He accepted. He was safe. At that moment in his mind he was already free. *"God helps those who help themselves,"* my dad kept repeating the statement like a mantra as he gave way to a demanding sleep.

The Run

Chapter 5

THE RUN

A few days after seeing all his relatives and friends being slaughtered like animals, my dad told us later, he decided to follow his heart and try to escape. So the very next time we went to visit my dad, he said to my mom, while she tenderly caressed his stubbly face, "I am a dead man, no matter how you look at it. There is no choice. I have to try for freedom. Remember," he smiled, "God helps those who help themselves." Those words got firmly inscribed into my brain forever.

"I am afraid for you," she whispered. "They will catch you and kill you," she continued with a soft cry. At that moment my mother realized that he was her whole life, and she did not want to go on without him. She had learned to love the man whom she accepted, because she had to.

My father's voice was firm, yet gentle. He held my mother's face in his cupped hands.

"Listen to me," he commanded. "You have to be strong. You have to save us." He paused and kissed her forehead.

"Call my sister, Laura, as soon as you get home. Have her watch the kids. Get a plain cotton scarf and cover your hair and most of your face. Don't wear any makeup or jewelry. You have to be strong, my love. You have to save us."

The panic, mixed with strength, filled my mother's consciousness as she realized that she held our four lives in her attitude.

I looked at my dad. He seemed different. He was energized, and he seemed more cautious than ever before. He had this weird look on his face, but I couldn't figure out what it meant. He kept whispering into my mother's ear. I wiggled myself between them, trying to catch the sound of their conversation, while my brother, Ike, just held on to my mother's coat, sniffling. My mother pulled my shoulder, telling me to be still. I started to ask questions, when my father put his hand on my mouth. "Now is not the time. You'll understand everything later. Don't talk and don't ask any questions. Just be still."

"Take your diamond bracelet," my father continued whispering. "Go to the Dorchol area where I had the grocery store, and ask if Jovan Ilich is still around. He used to have a print shop, and I know he won't turn you down. I also know you can trust him. But, do take the diamond bracelet, and ask him if he can make us false passports with Christian names."

A Nazi guard walked by us. My father stopped talking and kissed my mother. She seemed to have left the scene emotionally. My dad shook her. The Nazi returned and stood there staring at us. He spit a huge wad on the

ground next to us and moved on.

"I heard every word you said," my mother whispered.

The next day, we became Greek Orthodox Serbian Christians, and with the disguise of mustache, change of hairstyle, and glasses, the first leg to our plan for escape was established.

My name became Ijiljana Spasojevich. My mother became Anna Spasojevich. Ike became Ilija Spasojevich and my father became Svetislav Spasojevich.

Our next visit to the concentration camp included my aunt, Laura. At that time, a plan for escape was born.

"Take Danica, and go to my house at 2:30 tomorrow morning. Help Rachel with the kids." My father urged looking at his sister straight in the eyes. Then, he turned to my mother and continued. "Dress warmly. Don't take any luggage. Take your jewelry and the money."

He breathed heavy and talked disconnectedly, "Hire a fiacre, (horse and buggy) to come to the house at 3:00 A.M. Leave the house casually. Don't wake anybody up. Laura, you can go home. I don't think there will be immediate danger to women and children."

He then looked back at my mother and continued. "You will bring the children, tomorrow morning at 4 o'clock. Leave the children in the buggy, and go to that doorway across the street, and wait there for me." He pointed to a street and further explained about the doorway. "Don't talk to anybody. Don't tell the driver of the buggy where

you are going. You will be parked on the next block. He doesn't have to know. You don't want him to know. Offer him extra money, because it is so early in the morning. Have a babushka for you, and bring me an old hat and a coat."

As if in a daze, my mother just nodded. She seemed unable to talk.

"Go now," he said as he kept kissing all of us."I will see you tomorrow. Just know that I will. I have some planning and thinking to do until then."

We left the death camp. I looked at my mother, not daring to ask anything. I tried to figure out things from her face. *Was she happy, was she sad, what was she going to do, and how?* I just knew that I was not supposed to ask anything. When we got to the house, all the people who were still there, wanted to know how my father was and what was happening. I watched my mom to see what she would say. But, all she said was that everything was fine.

Then I watched her and Aunt Laura, as they disappeared into one of the bedrooms.

My mother woke me up at 2:30 the next morning. Aunt Laura and Danica stayed at our house overnight, and my aunt was still in her terrycloth robe and already feeding Ike breakfast. He sat in her lap, while she shoveled food into his mouth in spite of his objections. She put Ike on the chair and walked toward my mother. They embraced and held on to each other, crying. Aunt Laura kept reassuring my mother, who was still in a daze. But she did as father instructed. Aunt Laura, who still hadn't heard

from her husband since he left for the war, was happy to be with us and help save her brother's life.

Everyone thought that the war was going to be over before the Nazis started picking up women and children. It seemed that there wasn't as much urgency for Aunt Laura and her little baby to run as it was for us. We had to, because my father was attempting the impossible. He was escaping from the Nazi concentration camp.

Mom took his old coat and hat and put it in a bag. She took the little purse with money and a gold malay bag full of jewelry, which she stuck in her bra. She also took the snacks that Aunt Laura made for us. The rest of the people were still sleeping and it was very quiet. Not even Aunt Erna, or Uncle Ralph knew what was going on. I wanted to kiss my little cousin, but Aunt Laura did not want me to wake her up.

The fiacre came on time. It was still very dark and rainy. I hated getting up in the middle of the night. I hated the rain. But I knew we were going to meet my dad and that made it all O.K. We sat inside the carriage. The driver let down the side and front flaps of the carriage to protect us from the rain. We were glad about that, because that also protected us from being seen. Ike slept in mom's lap. I sat in the seat across from them. I was restless and I got up.

My mother told me to sit next to her and she put her arm around me. That felt warm and safe. She didn't do that very often. She always seemed to be concerned about Ike. I was just happy to have my daddy. He always made me feel safe. But that morning she was very nice to me. She even pulled me closer to her with her hand and brushed

my hair away from my wet face. I moved as close to her as I could and leaned my head against her arm. That made me very happy.

We didn't talk. We just dozed. I know that my mother prayed. After all, she did come from a very religious family in Nish, the small town in Serbia, Yugoslavia. Even though my mother did not want to marry my dad, he never gave up. He persisted and he always said that my mother was worth waiting for. He really loved her very much.

I think that my mother, being a snob, frequently thought that she could have done better, than to marry a grocery store owner. But, he had been good to her. She never had to do anything, or solve any problems. My dad took care of everything and everyone, and now she was helping him to save his life and ours.

We arrived at our destination, which was the side street, one block away from the camp. My mother put Ike on the seat and told me to watch him. She told the driver that no matter how long it took, for him to wait there for her, and then she was gone. She followed my father's instructions to a tee. By this time, the rain came down in torrents. I could hear the heavy drops of rain hit the leather top of the fiacre. (European buggy) I cuddled inside the buggy, and held Ike so tightly that he had to move in order to breathe.

And so we waited. And waited. And waited. I wanted to pray. I wanted to cry out. I wanted to scream at the mean Nazis for disrupting my life, and for taking my daddy away. But I knew he was going to be with us soon. I

rubbed my magic button, which I had cut out of my dads pajamas, and waited for my dad to appear.

In the meantime, at camp that evening, my dad's name came up for deportation.

"I am sorry, Danon. I saw your name on the list. They'll be collecting you soon," a man said to my dad.

It was minutes before they started to read the names of the doomed. My father's head started racing. *Kitchen. Office. Bathroom. Yes, bathroom. I cannot let them take me now,* my father thought, as he raced towards the bathroom. *I have life waiting for me tomorrow morning.*

He barely reached the bathroom when the echo of the names began to sound. My dad ran into the bathroom and flattened himself against the wall, behind the open door. He heard his name being called. He held his breath. And then he heard the footsteps. His name echoed throughout the entire camp. The sound of the footsteps became louder and crisper. He did not move. He held his breath.

A man poked his head into the bathroom, yelling, "Hey, Danon, are you in here? You are being called."

My father heard them calling his name but did not move. He put his fingers into his ears to cut out that horrible sound. He was inches away from the man who came looking for him. He was only seconds away from death. After a while, he heard the trucks pull away, laden with their human cargo, with life, which a loving God created and gave to them, and which was shortly to be extinguished by evil men exercising their free will.

63

When the excitement and the activities settled down, my father, feeling the absence of his body, slid along the wall, and spread himself on the floor.

"What the hell are you doing here?" a voice was shouting arousing my dad from inertia. "Don't you know that I am responsible for every man? Make sure to be out there the next time they call you!" he screamed with anger, as he left the bathroom and my dad sprawled on the floor.

My dad felt sorry for the man, but he certainly was not going to meet his own death, for him.

The second call came an hour later. My dad had no time to think or create a plan of escape. He was near the chicken coop, when he heard his name being called again. He looked around and dove right into the dirt and chicken poop and covered himself with it.

As before, Sam Danon, Sam Danon, echoed throughout the entire camp. He held his breath. No one came. No footsteps. Just his name echoing over and over and over. My dad did not move. He just lay there in the damp dirt, chicken poop and smelly straw.

How sweet life seemed at that moment. To be alive. To breathe. To feel your wife in your arms, and the softness and special scent of your children. How often we waste the time, being caught up in trivial things of absolutely no value, or importance. Or how we pay attention to what he said, what she said. How we trudged over unimportant events in our lives, as though our very lives depended on them.

Now, my father's life depended on his wit and quickness of thought. But, my father was always sure of himself. It was almost as though an invisible force or energy was guiding and protecting him. My dad did not move until he heard the trucks with their precious cargo drive off. One more time he was safe. He'd cheated death, at least for the moment. He knew that there was going to be one more call between now and tomorrow morning.

It was still raining and he was covered with mud. He wanted to go and change, but did not dare be seen.

"What are you doing here in the mud?" a man asked as he seemed to appear from nowhere. "Don't you know they are looking for you all over?"

"I fell here in the mud, and twisted my ankle. I can hardly move."

The man helped my dad to the barn, as my father dragged his foot along the muddy ground. He barely had time to wash and change, when they started calling the names again.

The calling and shipping out of men was accelerated, because the Nazis were bringing in more men from all over Yugoslavia and needed room for the newcomers. They needed to solve the Jewish problem. My dad panicked. He was afraid they would nab him this time. But he was going to outsmart them, one more time. One more call stood between life and death. He looked around. There was no place to hide. No furniture. No walls. Just straw and dirt and God. The hospital. He flashed on the hospital, which was only a few steps away.

He entered this creepy place called "hospital," and found his friend, the young doctor, whom he helped to see his mother.

"Quick Doctor, take a syringe, and if anyone enters, stick it in my arm. I am sure you can find a reason."

He showed my father to a filthy bed, and with one hand, he held my father's arm, and with the other, he took a syringe and held it. His hands were shaking. His face was ashen.

"I'll never forget what you did for me and my mother," he whispered.

"Sam Danon, Sam Danon. Sam Danon." My father's name echoed throughout the camp as before. Over and over and over. But no one came to the hospital, and my dad knew he made it. He walked out into the rain, looked up and let the gentle rain caress his face. "Thank You! Thank You! Thank You!" he whispered, as his tears blended with the raindrops and slid down his face.

"I am personally going to see that you are here tomorrow, when they call your name," the angry man shouted. "Don't you know that your caginess can cost me my life?"

How ironic, it could cost the man his life. My father felt bad for the Jewish sentry, but he was not about to run into the waiting arms of death.

My dad did not go to sleep that night. He had to think of a plan soon. He knew we would be waiting for him in the

early morning. He also knew this was his only and last chance for life. He followed his instincts. He trusted. He did not know how, but he knew it would be done. The night seemed to move slowly. My dad could not, or would not fall asleep. He wanted to smoke. He wanted to run. He wanted to take action. But he had to wait for the perfect timing. There could be no mistakes. Failure was not an option. There were no second chances in a concentration camp. He tossed and turned and shivered on top of the damp straw. He was cold and he was afraid. The gentle rain from this afternoon had turned into a heavy stream of water, making the visibility almost zero. My dad knew that this was the moment when the garbage truck would be waiting for him.

He walked alongside the truck and began collecting garbage, as usual. The rain seemed to come down in sheets, concealing the clarity of any and all movements within the camp. As my dad worked his way up to the camp garbage collector, he availed himself of the luxury of the smelly truck which moved freely within all the areas of the camp.

It was 3:30 A.M. My dad walked from one German cabin to another collecting garbage. His heart beat fast. He had to stop a few times to catch his breath. The garbage truck made its way to the German army kitchens. My dad was soaking wet as he ran alongside of the truck. From the kitchens, he took out large metal cans with smelly, rotted food leftovers from the Nazis.

One by one, my dad emptied the cans into the truck. The stench was unbearable. He was sure that there were human body parts in those cans.

When all the garbage was collected, and the rain furiously beat everything in its path, the truck started for the gate. My dad looked around. This was the moment of truth. There were very few guards out, and the ones that were there had their collars up to their ears, and hats pulled down, almost covering their eyes.

As the truck proceeded toward the gate, my dad dove into the truck bed and covered himself with slimy, smelly refuse, which had already started to disintegrate from all the rain. The truck started to move. It went through one section, where the wooden gates opened and closed. Then the truck went through another and another, while the German soldiers inspected every move of the truck. The truck came to the last section; the main gate and the barbed wire. As the truck arrived at the gate of the camp, my dad peered through the garbage, only to notice a guard at each side of the gate, inspecting every car and truck that came in or out.

The Nazis stopped the truck. One guard at each side, in spite of the rain. Each guard looked in the muck. My dad dug himself deeper into the slime, which by now was floating in the water, and he held his breath. The slime entered his nostrils, his ears and eyes. The truck idled at the gate. The heavy downpour made it difficult for the Nazis to see. The two guards pulled their coat collars over their ears and faces, looked in the cab of the truck where the driver was sitting, and motioned to the truck to exit.

The rain, like God's tears, protected and shielded my dad as he exited to safety and freedom. Outside the gate, the Nazi guard walked back and forth, guarding the gate.

When the truck was a few feet away from the gate, my dad jumped out, totally covered with slime. He had calculated the time it would take him to reach the doorway across the street, before the guard turned around.

"What if I take one step too many? What if the guard walks faster? What if the Nazi turns around and sees me running? I did not come this far to be shot! I will make it. I am free, I am free!"

The Nazi walked away from the truck and the gate with his back to my father. Suddenly, the Nazi turned around as though he heard a noise. My dad saw him turning around and stopped dead in his tracks. The heavy downpour seemed to have obstructed the Nazi's view, as he proceeded to walk away from the gate.

In ten seconds, my dad reached the doorway across the street, and in twelve seconds, he was holding on to my mother, in his newly found freedom.

My father recounted his feelings to us many times later on. Ike and I sat in the buggy and anxiously awaited our visitor, my dad, the head of our family. When my dad entered the fiacre, the driver let the cloth sides of the carriage down. I threw myself into my dad's arms. Never did I smell anything so sweet that smelled so foul.

*

The very next day, the Nazis detected my father's absence from the camp. Immediately, they went directly to my Aunt Laura's home.

"Where is he, Judenschwein? Where are you hiding him?" Nazis yelled at my aunt, Laura.

She just stood there paralyzed with fear, while the Nazis poked each pillow and bed with their bayonets. Two of them looked into every closet, while the third one questioned her, beating her with his pistol. His angry, loud voice echoed throughout the whole building.

The neighbors came and peered through the windows and quickly ran away in fear of being next. When she failed to produce my dad, the Nazi walked over to my aunt, who was still holding her crying, frightened baby, took out his pistol, looked at her face and pulled the trigger. She collapsed on the kitchen floor as my baby cousin dropped on the floor next to her, screaming. The Nazi looked at the baby and without any emotion, pulled the trigger once again, leaving them both to bleed to death on the kitchen floor.

After the Nazis left my aunt's apartment, the neighbors went back in. They found my aunt and her baby dead, but walked away frightened, just waiting to tell the story to anyone who would listen. Their bodies lay on the floor until the smell became too strong. At that time, the Nazis sent some prisoners to clean up the stench and throw away the bodies. The guilt for my aunt's death stayed with my father for the rest of his life.

Two weeks after my father's escape, three men tried to

escape, but they were caught and hung in the middle of the camp, and left hanging until their flesh started to rot. No one had ever escaped from the German death camp in Yugoslavia, except for my father. God did help him because he helped himself.

The Chase

Chapter 6

THE CHASE

It was still dark and the rain was beating on the leather of the fiacre. My father sat there with us and it felt like a miracle had occurred. There was so much to say, but no one talked. I wanted to ask if we were going home. I wanted to know where my dad was going to change and wash up. I wanted to ask so many questions, but I knew they would not answer me. I knew that the reason they wouldn't tell me was that they themselves didn't know where we were going to go. My mother came up with a few names and places, but none felt right.

"They would sure be joyous to report us," my father said as he leaned against the coach and closed his eyes. We all knew that anyone caught protecting or hiding Jews would be killed instantly.

My father told the driver just to drive, so we could get away from the Nazi beehive and the death camp. We drove and drove.

"Let's go somewhere!" I cried. "I am tired. And, I am hungry. And, you stink."

My father broke out in laughter. He was so happy to be alive that he didn't care about anything else.

"How would you like to give your father another big hug and a kiss?" he continued grinning.

"How can you joke at a time like this?" My mother complained.

I was so glad she intervened, because I really did not want to hug him again.

A Nazi car siren blew directly behind us. My mother put her hands on her mouth and opened her eyes in horror. My dad sat up and held his breath. The coach driver started to slow down until he came to a total stop. I heard the marching boots. My stomach started to hurt.

"Don't say a word," my father ordered all of us. "Where are the passports? You do have them?"

"Passports? Oh, my God. Where are the passports?" my mother repeated in panic. Then, without saying another word, my mother went into her bag and handed my father an envelope. His forehead, was beading with sweat, right through the dirt on his face. It was still raining.

The Nazi got out of his car, pulled up his collar and walked to our buggy. As he lifted the leather flap to look in, the odor from my father hit his senses. He backed off curling up his nose.

"Your documents!" he demanded.

My father, without talking, handed him our passports. The Nazi looked at the pictures, getting everything wet from the rain.

"Go home and take a bath," the Nazi exclaimed.

Another step toward freedom had been accomplished. When the Nazi left, my father poked his head out of the fiacre and yelled at the driver.

"Turn around and go full speed. I will give you further directions."

He sat down and with the most urgency he said, "They'll be back. They didn't realize who I was. We have to make a decision immediately They will be back. I know it. We have to come up with something, now."

My father had always helped people. He helped many of his friends start in business. He also helped a lot of young people to get started financially, and emotionally. He never asked for, or waited for a reward, because he knew it was his duty as a human being, to help those who had less than he.

My father was not a religious man, but I am sure he believed in cause and effect. He knew there was a law and an order in the universe, but had no clue how to explain what that meant.

In his leather goods store, my father employed a young, Serbian man. Dad had given him a job when he couldn't even buy food for his children. Bozidar was a nice, grateful man, but would he be willing to risk the lives of his family to save ours?

"Where does Bozidar live?" My father probed his memory. He poked his head out again, and gave the driver additional instructions and directions where to go. By this time, the driver was starting to get annoyed.

"I've been driving you all night I am not going to do this much longer, for the same money," he complained.

My father got out of the carriage, and climbed up next to the driver and negotiated a different price. As he started to get back in the carriage, he heard the Nazi siren again.

"Quick, turn into this small, dark street, and stop." He didn't want the Nazis to hear the hoofs of the horses echoing on the cobblestone street. We waited and waited. When the sirens stopped, we moved on. My parents were afraid that the Nazis stopped the sirens to pull us out of the hiding place, but they were truly gone.

The dawn was starting to show itself, but the streets were

still deserted. An hour later, we stood in front of Bozidar's house in the suburbs of Belgrade.

My father knocked at the door. There was no answer. He took one step back, wondering if Bozidar and his family were still living there, or were they even alive.

"It's early. They are still sleeping," my mother whispered. "Try again."

"Who are these people? Why would they let us in?" I thought. I wanted to go somewhere where we could sleep and eat and go to the bathroom. My father knocked again, gently. The lights came on in the front room, and then the door chains clanged, and the door opened.

"What the hell? Look at you!" Bozidar spoke as though he saw a ghost. "What the hell are you doing here? Don't you know?......"

"Can we come in? I'll tell you everything," my father interrupted.

"No, you can't come in. I am not going to risk my family. Do you want to have us all shot?"

"I don't want to have your family shot. I just want to save mine," my father spoke, as the tears ran down his face.

"Please, give us shelter. Please, save my family. Let us in just for one night. Please. Give us a chance at life," my father pleaded as my mother sobbed softly at his back.

"Wait a moment," Bozidar said, slamming the door in our faces.

"Aren't they going to let us in?" I asked.

By this time Ike, who was only eight years old started to cry. "I want to go home!" He was tired. He was hungry and he was cold.

We could hear voices coming through the door. They were arguing. "But the children. We must help them." Bozidar's wife pleaded with her husband. The door opened wide and they grabbed us and pulled us into the house.

"Just for one or two days," Bozidar said. "My wife's heart is bigger than her brain."

They gave all of us baths and dug up some old clothes. It felt good and it felt safe.

"Where were you? Why were you so dirty?" Bozidar kept asking, when we all sat around the table.

The table was covered with a red and white checkered tablecloth, made of some cheap plastic. I looked at the

squares and started scratching them with my fingernail. My father patted my hands, and told me to stop. I sat low in my chair, put my chin and my nose against the table cloth and smelled with a loud exhale. Seventy years later I can still smell that God awful, plastic tablecloth.

"I escaped from Sajmishte," my father said coldly.

"You mean Logor, the death camp? But this is unheard of!" Bozidar gasped standing up. "You have to leave now. Please just get up and leave."

Bozidar's wife walked to her husband's side, and put her arm around him.

"Let's feed them first, then they can leave." she said firmly. She brought out some homemade bread and butter, and a few slices of ham. My mother swallowed hard, but did not say a word. *"Thou shall not eat pork*," said a voice in her head.

"These are terrible times," Bozidar's wife said gently. "I am sorry I did not meet you earlier, when we were both happy. Bozidar told me a lot about both of you, and your beautiful store." She sat down and continued, "We sent the children to my mother's house. She lives in a small town and we thought it would be safer for them." Bozidar's wife was a little younger than my mother, and also very pretty. But all we could see was her big heart.

While we were eating, we heard a noise coming from outside. Everyone held their breath. It was just a car that drove by.

At the table my father and Bozidar talked about the store and the good old times. After we all had a bite, Bozidar said we could stay the night. He showed us the drill, what to do, in case someone should come to the door. He showed us, that in the middle of the living room, there was a Muslim Prayer rug. On the rug, sat a small round coffee table. Bozidar moved the table, then bent down and removed the rug, revealing a trap door in the floor. With some difficulty, he opened the trap door to show us an underground passage, similar to a sewer, low and narrow.

"If someone comes to the door, I want you all to jump in, and I will put the table back. There will be no questions or discussion. Do we understand each other?" Bozidar spoke, with authority.

"But how...." I started to ask, when my father put his hand across my mouth to shut me up. This was not a subject for discussion. The rules were set and there was no choice or option.

We all went to sleep without any incidents. I thought it was all over and I wanted to go home.

In the early morning, we were awakened by the pounding on the door. The prearranged drill came into effect. We all jumped off the couches, grabbed all evidence of our existence, and leaped into the sewer. Bozidar replaced the rug and the table, took a deep breath, and still in his nightwear, opened the door.

Two, three, four, five Nazis marched in. They were yelling in German, which Bozidar did not understand. They opened every closet. They opened every door. They ran their bayonets over and under the bedding.

A Nazi dressed in SS uniform, who was not German, but Croatian, said to Bozidar, "A kike escaped from the logor (death camp) and we are checking the whole town. We will find that pig Jew. He can't get away from us."

There was hate and fire in the Croatian's eyes, and Bozidar knew that the Croatian hated the Serbs, almost as much as he hated the Jews.

As they did not find us, the Nazis proceeded on to the next house.

Bozidar closed the door behind them, and collapsed on the floor. His wife, who up to now hadn't said a word, ran toward him and put her arms around him.

"We all could have been shot to death. I should never have let them in," Bozidar whispered. They could hear the Nazis abusing the household next door.

"But we are all still alive," his wife spoke softly. "And tomorrow, they'll be gone and we will have done the right thing."

In the meantime, we sat in the sewer. The space was small, so none of us could sit up straight. Ike was squirming in my mother's arms. My dad sat on his tailbone leaning against the wall, touching the ceiling with his head. I sat up. I felt like I was suffocating. There was no air in there. I changed my

position and hit the ceiling every time. My mother started to get annoyed, so my father pulled me against him and told me to go to sleep.

"I can't sleep," I protested. "I just woke up." I started to cry.

"Do you want to get us all killed?" my mother asked angrily. "Your father just got out, and you want him dead. Be still and don't hit that ceiling anymore." Our ceiling was the floor of the living room, and my mother didn't want me to make noise. I was bored. There was nothing to do and no one to talk to. My curious mind was aching for challenges, but life offered me nothing but fear and boredom. I swallowed hard. I didn't want my father dead. I put my head on his knee and cried myself to sleep. I don't know how much time passed, when we heard Bozidar open the hatch to our tiny space ship.

"They are gone, for now," he said, somewhat annoyed.

I sure was happy to get out, as I watched my parents crawl out, holding their backs.

We all sat around the table staring at each other, shaking with fear. "Will they return? Will they kill the Serbs because they couldn't find the Jews?" We heard of a German family who were all shot, because their younger son reported them for not embracing Nazi philosophy.

"You have to leave," Bozidar broke the silence.

"They will, but let's have some breakfast first," his wife said, as she put some ham and bread on the table.

When Bozidar and his wife left the living room, my parents looked at each other.

"Where? Where can we go?" My mother started to cry.

"We have the passports. We are Serbs now. We are Christians. We'll go with God. Don't worry. We'll make it. I promise. We'll make it."

"Why did they all hate the Jews?" I thought.*"Why did they hate us? We didn't do anything. We didn't hurt any one. What made us different from the Christians? And what were the Nazis thinking when they killed the Jews?"* I had so many questions and no answers and no one to talk to about it.

My mother looked at my father, making promises he wasn't sure he could keep, then at the ham on the table, and she couldn't decide which annoyed her more. She took a bite of bread and left the table.

I sat there with my chin resting on the smelly, disgusting red and white plastic table cloth. Only my eyes moved and observed. I was scared and didn't want my father to die. It sure would have been nice if my parents gave me a book to read, but at that time, they were not concerned with my education. They were concerned with just staying alive.

Another car drove by. Everyone stopped and listened. Bozidar and his wife returned to the living room and peeked out the window.

"You have to leave, before I go crazy," Bozidar cried out.

"We will, I promise. Just give us a little more time and

hopefully the Nazis will stop looking for us." My father motioned to my mother. They went into the bathroom together.

"What jewelry do we have left?" my father asked my mom.

My mother pulled the little pouch from her bra, opened it and showed it to my father. He reached in and took out a white gold watch surrounded with diamonds. He looked at my mom, who just nodded in agreement.

"We want you to have this," my dad said to Bozidar and his wife. We don't have much money left, but please accept this as our token of gratitude."

Both Bozidar and his wife said they didn't want anything, as their hands automatically reached for the magnificent timepiece. Bozidar's wife put on the watch and gave a big hug to my mother.

"We would have taken you in even without any payments," she said, "We will never forget how kind your husband was to us, when Bozidar just got started."

One day turned into two, and two into three, and so on for one week. We hid in the sewer a few more times, but none of us ever left the house.

One morning my parents read in an underground newspaper about the Jews in Italy. Benito Mussolini, the Italian dictator, had created an internment camp in Ferramonti di Tarsia, located in southern Italy. Even though it was a concentration camp, it was nothing like the German ones. The internees could receive mail and food, and they had a synagogue in the

camp. They also had a school and a theater. When Hitler asked Mussolini to turn over all the Jews to Germany, he refused. There was talk that Mussolini, at one time, had had a Jewish girlfriend. The Ferramonti camp was started in 1940, and it was disbanded in August of 1943. Almost all of the 3,600 Jews collected were foreign born, not Italian.

As he read the article about the Italian's treatment of Jews, my father decided that we would make our way to Italy. He wasn't sure how we would get there, but at least he had a plan.

Bozidar and his wife gave us some old clothes, a basket full of food, and hugged us goodbye. We all knew that we would never meet again, but we also knew that God put them on our path, like a bridge or a stepping stone, to save us, and guide us into our new lives.

We walked out of the house and hired the first horse and buggy that drove by.

"Take us to the railroad station," my father ordered.

Mostar

On River

Neretva

Chapter 7

MOSTAR ON RIVER NERETVA

With our new identities, and passports to match, we proceeded to the railroad station. Again, we encountered mobs of people going in all different directions. We were all scared, but we were lost in the sea of people, which made it a little easier. The Croatians were leaving Belgrade, Serbia and going to Croatia and Dalmatia. The Serbs, in turn, were coming in droves from Bosnia and Croatia. It appeared to be a voluntary ethnic cleansing. Children were crying and most adults were screaming at each other.

We made our way to a railroad car, which was not destroyed by bombs, and pushed our way in. It was a box car with straw on the floor. It smelled like animal poop. I started making faces. My father's hand went over my mouth.

"Don't say a word." he said.

I swallowed my complaint.

We had barely sat on the floor, when the Nazis came in, asking for our papers.

"Oni su Zidovi," (They are Jews) a toothless old woman,

with a head scarf, cried out. The Nazi either didn't hear her, or did not understand her, so he ignored her.

"They are Jews!" she screamed again. The Nazi turned around to see what she was saying, when an alarm came on. The train stopped.

My mom and dad looked at each other without a word, but there was panic on their faces.

"What is going on?" someone cried out.

"The Nazis have been looking for weeks for someone who ran away," a voice volunteered.

"Ran away where?" another voice came up.

I was scared. *Were they looking for my father? For us?* I thought, in a panic. My stomach hurt. I had to go to the bathroom, but I didn't dare say a word. Two different Nazis came back and asked us for our passports. By this time the ugly woman was gone. My father handed the Nazis our passports. He flipped through the pages, comparing our faces to the pictures on the small blue booklet. He handed us the passports and moved on to the next person.

My mother held her breath. When the soldiers moved on, she almost fainted. She closed her eyes and leaned her head against my father's shoulder.

"Shema Israel," she murmured under her breath. The train started again. The voices on the train calmed down. The children, with the lull of the train, started to fall asleep. My father took a deep breath, and leaned back against the wall of

the train, but never, at any time did he close his eyes completely. I wasn't sure how much time elapsed when the train started to slow down again.

"Where are we?" my mother asked, opening her eyes.

I looked at Ike, practically glued to my mother. How I wished she would hold me like that. But then, I was grateful I had my father who loved me.

I remember many times when Ike was picking on me, and mother would come and without even asking what happened, she would slap me for starting a fight with my little brother. I should know better, she would say. I never figured out what it was that I should know.

This love of sons over daughters stemmed from the period when daughters had to have a dowry in order to marry. And if a man had too many daughters, he could go broke giving them dowries. The sons were a prize in any man's household. The sons were also considered bread earners.

The train stopped and the voices became louder, one more time. A Nazi came aboard making his way between sleeping bodies on the floor of the train. He sometimes kicked the sleepers, causing them to cry out. This time the Nazi walked directly to us, asking for our passports.

"Bist du ein Jude?" (Are you Jewish?) he asked my father.

"Nein, Ich bin ein Serbe. Ich bin Christlich-Orthodox," my father answered. "No, I am a Serb. I am a Christian."

"And you?" he continued, looking at my mother.

"This is my wife, and she is Serbian also," my father intervened.

"Shut up! Shut up, you pig!" the Nazi shouted at my father.

"I... I... I am Serbian," she muttered.

The Nazi looked at the pictures on the passports, again, and continued his inquisition.

"Where are you going?"

"Our house was destroyed by bombs" my father thought quickly. "We are going to look for our relatives in Mostar."

It appeared that the Nazi was not going to let up, when a civilian came up to him and whispered something close to his ear. The Nazi threw the passports at us, and turned around and walked away.

As soon as the Nazi was out of sight, my dad got up yanked my mother off the floor, grabbed me by the arm, and pulled us to the other end of the train, where we all jumped off and ran into the fields.

The first thing I did, was to squat and pee. My mother handed me a piece of newspaper, and said, "Here, wipe yourself off."

As soon as we were a safe distance from the train, we sat on some rocks and ate the food Bozidar's wife packed for us. The sun was setting, and the air had started to cool off. We walked and walked, until we saw a house. Boldly, but politely, my father knocked on the door. A man opened it. He

seemed angry.

"What do you want?" he asked, screaming, scaring me.

"Is there a way we could spend the night in your house? My wife and my children are cold and tired."

"There is no room," the man exclaimed, starting to shut the door in our faces.

"Please, mister. Just give us a small corner of a room. Please let us in. We are very cold." my father pleaded.

"What do you have in that bag?" the man asked, softening a little.

"I have half a ham and you can have it," my father said opening the bag. The man stepped outside and looked around. Then he reached into the bag and took the ham.

"All right, but just for tonight."

He led the way to a semi-dark room that was full of people. They were all sitting on the floor occupying their own little space. When we entered, all eyes were directed at us.

The air in the room was cold and foul. It smelled like a clogged toilet. We stood in the entry for a few seconds. We saw a space against the wall and walked over there, between the bodies already seated, and sat down. My dad put an arm around my mother, who was holding Ike, sat me between his legs, and with his free hand, he opened a pocket knife and held it, in a ready-for-action position.

We did not know who those people were, or if they were going to kill us during the night, and take what we had. It was not unusual, during that period of time, to kill a person for the shoes on their feet.

We all fell asleep, except my father. A lot of people in the room were snoring. My mother woke up and needed to use the bathroom. A person pointed to an area behind the curtain. I got up with her. She took Ike by one hand, and me by the other, as we walked to the back, behind the curtain. To my horror, I recognized where that horrible smell was coming from. There on the floor, was a chamber pot overflowing with urine, and next to it, another bucket full of feces. I pulled my hand from my mother, and backed up.

"I am going,"she said releasing my hand. She took Ike and showed him where to pee. He thought it was very funny to see all that shit and urine all over the place. He enjoyed aiming into the pot and laughed real hard when he missed.

As soon as it started getting lighter, we got up off the floor and made our way out into the cold air one more time. We pulled our measly attire closer to our ears and started marching in the direction of Mostar.

In the 16th Century, Mostar was the chief administrative city for the Ottoman Empire. Consequently, most of it's inhabitants were Muslims. What Mostar was mainly known for, was the Old Bridge, which was the most important symbol of the Ottoman Empire. It took nine years to build, and it was completed in 1566. It was a single span, stone arch, that became a world heritage site. Artists from all over the world went to Mostar to paint the famous bridge.

My dad thought that Mostar would be just big enough for us to get lost in. And, he also knew that there was a Serbian Orthodox Church, which was built in 1881. We felt very comfortable in the company of Serbs.

We walked for maybe an hour, when a band of men surrounded us. They grabbed my dad and pulled his arms back. My mother started to scream, when one of the men stuffed his dirty handkerchief into her mouth. He put his knife to her throat and softly whispered, "You make one more sound, and I will cut your pretty little throat." He spoke Serbian.

The fellow who was holding my father started asking him questions.

"Who are you? Where are you going? Do you have any money?" The questions were so close together, that my dad didn't have time to answer any of them. The man looked at me and Ike.

"Are these your children?"

"And who are you?" I heard myself ask. Neither my dad nor my mom could put their hand over my mouth, so I was free to express my curiosity.

The fellow looked at me and burst out laughing. "Bold little thing, aren't you?"

"We are Cetnici. We are the partisans. We fight with Tito."

By this time, he knew that we were no danger to them, so they removed the stuffing from my mother's mouth, and

released my father's hands.

"Then, you know my cousin, Mosha Piade?" my mother asked with joy.

"You mean Tito's right hand? Mosha Piade, the Jew?" one of the guys asked, surprised.

"Yes, that's the one!" my mother shook with joy.

"We are the real heroes of World War II. We are on the side of democracy and human values. We are anti-Fascist Yugoslavian Partisans, and we fight with Josep Broz Tito and Mosha Piade" He was standing tall and proud, like he was giving a speech.

Tito was part Croatian and Slovenian, and he was married to a Serbian woman. He was fair to all nationalities. With his iron fist of gentle Communism, he was the glue that held all the provinces in Yugoslavia together. They asked us when was the last time we ate, gave us some chocolates and bread, and hugged us goodbye.

"I didn't know Mosha Piade was your cousin," my father asked.

"He is not!" my mother laughed.

"But over there you told them he was your cousin."

"It worked, didn't it?" she laughed out loud, which she had seldom done since the war started. "I heard my parents talk about him often, but I didn't think we were related."

The sun started to set, and once more we were faced with the dark and the cold. The partisans had given us good directions to Mostar and we were finally on our way. It must have been close to 10:00 PM, when we saw the first house. If it hadn't been so cold, it might have been fun walking through the narrow streets of Mostar. The houses were small, quaint and white washed. Some had tiny gardens in front with white picket fences.

Without knowing where or why, we walked to a house and knocked at the door. A faint light came on in a window, the curtain moved, but no one came to the door.

"I guess we were not expected," my father said jokingly.

We walked a bit longer and knocked at another door. Again, a light came on, a curtain moved, but this time a woman's voice came through the door."What do you want?"

I could tell she was old, because her voice was shaking.

"We are looking for a place to spend the night. My children are cold and hungry." my father said.

The curtain opened wide, and an old face with missing teeth appeared, framed in the window pane. She must have approved of us, because the door opened wide and she showed us in.

"It will cost you. I do nothing for free. Nobody gives me nothing for free. That no good husband of mine never gave me nothing."

At first, she scared me a little, and then I thought she was

funny looking. She was short and fat, and she talked too much. She wore a scarf on her head, like most Muslim women. Her living room was funny looking, too. There were Persian rugs on the floors, like we had in our house in Belgrade, and there were wall to wall couches, and funny material covered her ceilings and walls. In front of one couch there was a round, brass coffee table.

"How much money do you have?" she asked, dancing around us, staring at my father's hands.

My dad looked at my mother.

"Not much left," my mother said pensively. She turned away from the old hag, reached down into her bosom, and pulled out what was left of her only possessions. She took out a cameo brooch and handed it to my dad.

"We don't have much, and we have no money. But you can have this brooch, if you let us stay here for a week."

The old lady grabbed the brooch from my dad's hands, took it under the light and nodded. "You can stay here for a week, but don't ask me to give this back to you. Where is your luggage?" she asked looking around.

"We have nothing. We need very little." my mother spoke softly, almost in tears.

The old lady patted my hair. "Poor little thing," she said as she led us upstairs, to a bedroom. The room was small and crowded. There were two beds and two dressers of drawers, a tall one and a shorter one.

She told us we could use the taller one, but not to touch the shorter one. There was a small gas burner and a pot on the table near the bathroom. The table had a drawer holding some old silverware. She told us we could make coffee or whatever on the burner.

No sooner did the old lady close the door behind her, when I jumped off the bed, and tried to open the drawers of the shorter dresser.

"Didn't you hear what the lady said?" my mother said, as she pulled me away from the dresser.

"Yes, but I want to know what is in there."

"It is none of your business, what is in there. She was kind enough to let us use the room and you will respect her wishes."

"Yes, but, but..."

"Nothing but! Wash your hands. Here is a piece of bread. Eat it, and go to sleep." My mother was firm. She also gave Ike a piece of bread and he demanded butter. There were only a few more crumbs left, which my parents split and we all went to sleep hungry. This was the first time, since the bombs fell, that my father allowed himself to go into a deep sleep.

I woke up early the next morning and ran to the window. The sun was just starting to come up and the sky was all red and pink and blue. It was gorgeous. The light reflected on the multitude of red tile roofs. I cried out with joy so loud, that I scared both my parents and Ike.

"Is someone hurting you?" Ike asked rubbing his eyes.

One of my parents told me to go back to sleep.

How could I go back to sleep when there was so much to explore? I thought. The first thing I had to do, was to find out what was in those drawers. I was bursting with curiosity. I tried to open one. It was locked. I pulled on the handle again and again. It would not open. I looked around the room. I found a spoon. I stuck it in the hole, where the key was supposed to go, and I heard a click. I pulled on the handle again, and like magic, it opened. I looked in. Disappointment filled me. There were some old paper bags filled with lima beans.

"Lima beans!" I screamed. It must have been loud, because both my mom and dad sat up in the bed. I don't know what I expected, but it certainly wasn't lima beans.

"Now you are in trouble," my father said as he sat in bed. "You disobeyed me, and dishonored the old lady. What am I going to do with you? Your curiosity is beyond control. Come here. Sit down." He said making room on the bed next to him. "If this were Ike, doing what you just did, how would you punish him?"

Without even thinking, I screamed out all excited. "I would make him eat those horrible lima beans."

"Brilliant, just brilliant. Your mother is going to cook those horrible lima beans, and you are going to eat them," he said smiling.

We all took baths; wonderful, lukewarm baths, and put on

the same dirty old clothes, because that was all we had. My mother took out the one pot that was in the room, put in some water and lit the gas etna, then she took some lima beans from the drawer, put them in the pot and started cooking them. She found salt and pepper in the table drawer and the old beans became a delicacy.

I was very hungry and I actually looked forward to tasting the beans, until I looked in the pot. There, on the top of the boiling water, swam what must have been hundreds of worms. I wanted to run away, but there was no place to run. We were the prisoners of the room and the fat old lady.

"It's a shame to throw it all out. I don't know when we will have food again," my father said somberly.

"But the worms. We can't eat the worms," my mother cried.

"We are not going to eat the worms," he said, taking a spoon, and scooping them out, and throwing them in the toilet.

"I don't like worms," Ike objected. "Do I have to eat worms?"

"Worms are instead of meat," my dad laughed. It was so good to hear my dad laugh, that I didn't care about the beans or worms, or any kind of food. I ran into my father's arms and gave him the biggest hug I could manage.

"I am so glad you are here, Daddy."

We ate the beans. Most of the worms were out, but we laughed so hard, that the beans and the worms became irrelevant.

Then, my dad said, "Let's go downstairs and see if I can make some money, unless you want to eat the beans, again."

The old lady was sitting in her living room. She seemed to be smoking, but she was sucking on a contraption and blowing out smoke. She was drinking black coffee with a sugar cube in her mouth.

"Do you think there is some kind of work I can get? I need to make some money for food," my dad asked. He talked to the old lady, while we all chuckled in the back of the room.

"Can you chop wood?" she asked between puffs.

"There is a first time for everything," my father mumbled. "Of course, I can," he said, in a loud voice. She showed him where the wood and the ax were, and he went to work.

When she came back in the room, she turned to my mother and asked her to clean the kitchen. My mother was stunned. She never even talked to the maids that way.

"Of course I can, but I don't do it for free," she said, hardly containing herself from laughing.

The kitchen was a mess. There were dirty dishes, food scraps, newspapers and trash everywhere. Not being used to such a mess, my mother stood there as if paralyzed, looking.

"This is not going to get any easier," she said to herself. She rolled up her sleeves, looked at her nails, found a garbage can and started throwing everything out.

A few hours later, my mother looked around the kitchen. She

liked it. It felt good. She could do this. It's true that she was used to always having a clean house, but this time it was her accomplishment, not the maid's. She felt good about herself.

While she looked around, the old lady came in. "I think I like having you here," she said, and walked out of the kitchen.

In the meantime, my father came in with an armful of chopped wood, and stacked it up in the living room by the fireplace. The old lady paid him the agreed amount and even gave my mother some change for cleaning the kitchen.

"Let's go to town," my father said, excited. My parents took me and Ike by the hands, and we went into town. We walked the narrow, charming streets lined with cobble stone. We passed by quaint little houses and nearly empty shops. Our street took us directly to the famous Old Bridge, where young men from the village were diving into the river Neretva for money.

"Can we see them dive, please, Daddy, please?" I begged.

My father put his hand into his hip pocket and took out the necessary change for the boy to dive off the bridge. My mother thought we were extravagant for spending the few cents we had for unnecessary things.

"Don't worry, Sweetheart, there is lots more where this came from. Besides, God always provides what we need."

I found it very exciting to watch the young boys dive off the bridge, into the river. As we continued walking, we passed by what appeared to be a coffee shop, which was kind of bare. There were a few fancy cookies in the counter and coffee. My father looked at the cookies, and then at my mother.

"It couldn't be," she said.

"Why not?" my father responded, with his heart beating fast.

"They would take the same route as we did."

"Who makes these cookies for you?" my dad asked the store keeper.

"Some man brings them in a box. I pay him. I don't know who he is. Sometimes his wife brings them in, so I pay her," the store keeper said. "Do you want to buy one?"

My father looked at the little change he just earned, then at his family, and said, "We will take two of these." He split the cookies in half, and we had a feast.

"Where can I find this man?" my dad asked, again.

"I just told you, I don't know who he is, or where he lives. I don't even know his name. I think he is from somewhere in Serbia."

I licked my cookie, to make it last longer. I also looked at it between each lick. It was delicious, but not enough. We continued walking down the narrow cobble stone street, when we heard a high pitched, witch-like voice behind us.

"These are the people who knocked at my door last night. I am sure they are Jews!" a woman in her sixties danced around two men dressed in civilian attire.

They both wore fezzes and they were tall with heavy black mustaches. They looked like they might be local police. They were certainly either Turkish, or Muslim.

Were these Muslims the ones who worked with the Nazis? we wondered.

We knew that an uncle of Arafat, the Grand Mufti of Jerusalem, Haj Amin el-Husseini, recruited Bosnian-Muslim troops, which he personally delivered to Hitler. We did not know this policeman's feelings, and we were scared.

"May we see your papers?" one of them said politely.

The same fear we experienced with Nazis, was back. There was an inherent hate between the Muslims, Croatians and Serbs. They killed each other, just because their great grand parents killed each other, hundreds of years ago.

My father took out our passports and gave them to the local policemen. They looked at the pictures, then at us.

"What are you doing here? Why did you leave Serbia?" one of them asked.

"Our house was destroyed by the bombs. We have a relative here in Mostar, who we are trying to find," my father said, trying to keep calm.

"They tried to break into my house, last night," the dancing, toothless wench screeched.

"Go have another glass of wine," said the cop, as he sent her off. "What is your relative's name?"

Now my father was in a dilemma, because we had no relatives in Mostar, and these cookies may not have been made by my aunt and uncle. And we had no names to give to the police.

"My uncle makes the best cookies," I cried out, still licking the last crumbs of my cookie.

"You mean that skinny Serb, with the fat wife, is your relative?"

"Yes! That's the one," my mother answered, as if just having awakened from a dream.

"They live in the little green house, down the street." the local cop said. "You are right, little girl, they do make the best cookies. Go. Go see your relatives," the cop told us, as they both turned around and looked at the toothless woman.

"When will you stop making trouble? These are nice people. Now, go home and sleep it off, before I put **you** in jail."

In a dream of disbelief and excitement, we practically flew to the little green house. My father knocked on the door, while we all held our breath.

"It can't be. It can't be. That's impossible!" my mother mumbled.

"This would not be the first miracle we experienced in this war," my father said, almost arrogantly. He always came from a positive approach.

We waited. He knocked again. It felt like a year passed between knocks. The curtain on the window moved. A face of a woman appeared. Then a scream. The door opened wide, and the tears flew. The tears. The hugs. The screams. Then, prayers of gratitude.

"How? When? How did you? I thought they killed you in the concentration camp," my uncle exclaimed.

Everyone was asking questions and no one had a chance to answer anything. The two cops had followed us to see if we were telling the truth. They stood at a distance, and just watched with pleasure, the reunion of lost relatives.

"I see you met our friends," my uncle said, composing himself, and waving to the local cops. "They come here for coffee and cookies almost every morning."

"Do they know?" my father asked.

"Probably. But, they never ask any questions. They don't hate the Jews."

At an early age, I learned that there were two kinds of people in this world, those who hate Jews, and those who don't.

Surviving Is A Job

Chapter 8

SURVIVING IS A JOB

We all cried with joy. We hugged and we kissed. The rest of the day was spent catching up, in gratitude for this miracle. Aunt Erna fed us a good meal, and then she let me play with her hair while she talked with my parents. She had tar black, shiny hair and milk white skin.

"But how, when, how did you get here?" my mother asked, in amazement.

"When you, Sima, were picked up and taken to the death camp, we thought we would be next," Uncle Ralph started to tell us with excitement.

"We went to the railroad station and got on the only train that was not destroyed by the bombs," my aunt interrupted.

"But the papers, the passports? Did you get Serbian names? What did you do about that?"

"We heard of this man in Belgrade, who used to be a printer, and that he created false passports. So we went there, got the

papers, and got on the train, the only train that ran, and we got off here, at Mostar. We left everything. After the Nazis shot our Lucy and her puppies, we had nothing to hold us there," my aunt continued, wiping her eyes with the back of her hand.

"Did you hear what happened to Laura?" my father asked.

"Our poor sister helped you escape, so they, the Nazis went to her house, and shot her and her baby. A neighbor found them on the floor dead, drained of all blood."

My uncle started to choke and cough. He was very thin and delicate. My aunt got up and put her arms around him pressing his head against her breast. She took such good care of her beloved.

"I heard that the Nazis were taking all the Jews to Poland and Germany to some camp, where they kill them, or burn them all to death," my mother said, between sobs. "I know nothing of my family from Nish. My poor dad, he was so religious. He was such a good person and that's how he ended."

"I don't understand, why don't the Americans bomb that railroad that takes the Jews to the camps?" my uncle sobbed.

"President Roosevelt has bigger problems than the Jews," my father answered. "Besides, he does not want to be labeled as a Jew lover."

"Dead. Everyone's dead. We have no more family. No more nieces. No more nephews. Those poor, little, innocent children. All dead. Gone from the face of this earth. How

can God allow this to happen? I wonder if there even is a God?" my uncle cried, out loud, as his tears ran down my aunt's bosom.

"It isn't God that does these terrible thing to us. It is man, exercising his free will, and that's why God helps those who help themselves." My father got up and went to my mother's side.

She was crying hysterically. He pulled her up from her chair and held her. Ike and I looked around and burrowed ourselves between our parents. We both cried.

I wasn't exactly sure why I was crying this time, but my tears, with a mind of their own, just poured down my cheeks. It felt like I cried because my parents cried, and they had just said goodby to all the members of our family.

WHERE DID THEY ALL GO?

I stand alone.

Yesterday they were all here.

Today they are all gone.

They are all dead.

Brothers, sisters, cousins.

All dead.

Slaughtered, gassed, burned.

Why did I survive?

What did God want me to do?

What is the purpose for my life?

How can I serve Him?

And why did He allow this to happen?

He did nothing.

He said nothing.

He just cried in pain for His creation.

No one said a word for a long time. My uncle got up, went to the sink, and washed his face.

"Where are you staying?" he asked, breaking the spell of silence.

"At a fat lady's house," my father broke a smile.

"Oh, the widow. Her husband left her some money. She is not bad. She often rents rooms to supplement what she has. But I want you to come and stay here with us." my aunt said.

My mother looked around. The room was not too small, but it was full of furniture, plus a work table where my uncle made cookies.

"We already agreed with our fat lady to stay there for a week. Maybe we can find a place that is a little larger for all of us," my mother said.

"That sounds more logical," my uncle agreed. "We just don't want to let you go, ever again. We are the only ones that survived."

We all hugged and cried again, and then we left for our own castle in the sky, with the lima beans with worm protein.

Every morning, my father helped the old lady with the fire wood, and my mother straightened up the kitchen. Every afternoon, we went to my uncle's house, where he and my father made cookies, which they sold to different coffee houses. My mother and my aunt delivered the cookies.

"I hear the German army is pushing inward," my uncle said

one day. "They may be here soon. Maybe we should start thinking about moving on."

The fear and panic filled me again. I looked for the bathroom. My nervous stomach always knew when I got scared. *"Are they going to come here and take my dad again?"* I panicked. I ran into my father's arms, where I held onto him for dear life.

"They are not going to take you away again, are they Daddy?" I cried.

"No one is taking me anywhere." my father caressed my hair. "This time we are prepared. We will be a step ahead of them. We know what they are capable of. Failure is not an option. We will survive."

My dad and my uncle started making inquiries as to what kind of transportation we could get to Italy. We knew that Catholic nuns had taken in, hidden, and saved many Jews. But we also knew that the Italians were guarding their borders zealously.

We couldn't find anyone who would take all six of us toward the part of Yugoslavia which was occupied by the Italians, so we decided to separate just for the trip. The plans were laid for our reunion in Split. My father found a man who was willing to take only the four of us toward Split, on the Adriatic coast.

The author's father's identification papers.

We went to our room, and packed the few things we had accumulated. As we were ready to go downstairs and say goodby to our fat lady, of whom we had grown fond, my father sat me on his knee, and told me that I had some unfinished business. *What kind of business did I have,* I wondered. He looked very serious, and I didn't like that at all.

"Do you think it would be a good idea to pay our friend?"

"The fat lady," I interrupted.

"Yes, the fat lady," my father continued. "Don't you think it would be a good idea to apologize to her and pay her for the lima beans we ate?"

"We all ate them," I objected defensively.

"Yes, we all ate them, but who disobeyed her and opened the drawer?"

"I didn't mean to!" I cried.

"Yes you did," my father continued. "You meant it. So, I'll tell you what we'll do. You apologize to her for opening the drawer, and I will pay for the beans we all ate. How does that sound?"

I did not like apologizing, but I knew my father was right. He always knew the right thing to do. He was so smart, my daddy.

When we got downstairs, she was waiting. My father put his hand on my head, and steered me toward our friend.

"My daughter has something to tell you," my father said.

"I am sorry I opened your drawer," I mumbled.

"Louder, she didn't hear you," my father repeated.

"I am sorry I opened the drawer," I yelled out.

"What drawer?" The fat lady asked puzzled.

"The drawer with the lima beans," my father said. We ate some, and I want to pay you for them."

"Were those old things still in the drawer?" she asked. "Why that rascal! My husband couldn't stand lima beans, so he hid them from me, in his chest of drawers. Why, they must be years old!" the old lady laughed. "Thank you for solving the mystery of the lima beans for me. And no, I don't want you to pay me anything. I just wish you could stay longer. I will miss you," she said, wiping the tears from her eyes.

The horse and buggy were already outside waiting. But to our surprise, the buggy was a flatbed with straw on it. That is not what we contracted for, but it was a way to get us out. The driver wanted to get paid in advance, so my father took care of him before we climbed on the straw. I could feel the cold January wind blow right through me. We had no blankets or warm clothes.

"We might as well relax," my father said. "It's going to be a long ride.

My mother stretched out, and shielded Ike from the cold with her body. My father did the same next to her, shielding me

from the wind. We all fell asleep trying to escape the conditions. We rode for a long time when suddenly the cart stopped and backed up. It stopped and backed up, again. We were stuck in the mud. The driver yelled and beat the horse, but the cart seemed to have a mind of its own, and did not move. At that point, the driver decided that the weight in the cart was too much and he ordered us to get down. I looked at the mud below the cart. It was thick and deep. My mother also looked down.

"We can't walk in that," she complained.

But the driver was insistent, because he, too, had no choice. We got off the cart and stepped into the thick, gooey mass which grabbed our shoes and would not let go. The driver, after a few attempts, pulled the cart out and just kept going. We all screamed at him, but our words fell on deaf ears. He drove off with our food, and the few things we had bought in Mostar.

So there we were, in the middle of nowhere, stuck in the mud. With a lot of difficulty, we made our way out, but the mud still stayed on our shoes and legs. We walked through the fields not knowing where we were going. I was hungry. We all were hungry, but the driver of the cart had our food. We were hungry most of the time, and had all lost a lot of weight. There were no houses and no stores to buy anything.

Our walk seemed endless, and my stomach was gurgling. We passed by a field where they grew tomatoes. And there, on a little dried branch, was a tomato skin, swaying in the wind. I ran toward it. I bent down, and snatched it off the branch and stuck it into my mouth. A feeling of guilt came over me for not sharing it with my family.

My father called to me. He didn't like me taking side trips. Having just lost all his family, he did not let any of us out of his sight. We were all tired, cold and hungry, but we kept on walking, and walking, and walking.

The sun had warmed up the air some, but now it was starting to set. We walked a bit longer, when we saw the Italian carabiniere. There we were at the border, the four of us physically beaten and emotionally spent. We wore dirty, smelly clothes, draped over our skeletal bodies. Our only hope for survival was to cross over to the Italian side. We had no food, no money, no shelter, only hope. The setting sun cast a magnificent opalescent pink with shades of blue and gold. It seemed like God had lit up the skies, urging us on with all His Glory.

We got off the road, while my parents devised a strategy for crossing to the Italian side. For a moment, my parents stared at each other. In silent agreement, my mother took out the dirty little gold pouch from her bra, pulled open the strings and took out a ring with a huge diamond. Its brilliance created a multicolor rainbow, when she turned it to the setting sun.

There he was. Tall and slim, with a triangular hat. The Italian guard walked from one side of the road, to the other, guarding the entrance to Italian occupied Yugoslavia. He did that over and over. Occasionally, he stopped and stretched and yawned.

My mother put the ring into her hand and made a fist. With the other hand, she replaced the pouch back into her bra. She walked toward the carabiniere. She was only 32, but she looked older. And even with her dirty, muddy clothes, she

walked tall and proud. There was something regal about her. In that moment her spirit and her glow overcame the mud, and she was young, and she was beautiful.

She walked to the carabiniere, and without saying a word, she put the ring in his hand. For a moment, he was stunned, but then he looked at the ring. It radiated many brilliant colors, as he looked at it in his hand. He squeezed his hand, shut it, and turned his back to my mother. Quickly, she motioned to us to join her. We jumped out of the ditch, into the setting sun and the frame of God's glorious Light, and crossed the border to Italian occupied Yugoslavia.

Out of nowhere, houses appeared, lining the narrow cobble stone streets. The whole city seemed like an old fortress.

"This is beautiful, but can we stop somewhere? I can't go any further," my mother said, almost in tears.

My father jingled some change, which our fat lady paid him, and said, with a smile, "Anything you desire, my queen. We are rich." My dad always made light of things.

He also had a few dinars, which he had earned with Uncle Ralph's cookies. As before, we found a room, bought some food, took baths and went to sleep. Just as I fell asleep I felt something itching my legs. Then my back, until I felt a little bump on my stomach. I pulled on it only to find that we were infested with bed bugs which smelled real bad when popped. I also heard my parents and Ike sigh, turn and scratch.

The next day we found another room. The room was on the second floor, and the houses were so close together, that I

could see inside the house across the narrow street.

About midnight, I was awakened by sounds of laughter. It sounded like a drinking party. I got out of bed trying not to wake up Ike or my parents and ran to the window. I had to see what was going on. The window across the street was open with lights on and there were lacy curtains swaying in and out. The climate in Split was warm, so it was not unusual to have all the windows open. I moved our curtains out of the way, stuck my head out the window, and looked inside our neighbor's window. I didn't quite understand what was gong on, but I knew I had to watch. There was an Italian officer in his uniform, kissing a woman in her negligée. She was laughing, and wiggling. Just when I thought it was getting interesting, I felt my father's hand on my shoulders.

"Shame on you," he said, directing me back to bed.

"What did I do," I protested.

"You are not supposed to look in other people's windows." my father said, annoyed.

I went to bed, but I couldn't sleep. I found the sounds from the next building very disturbing.

We spent the next few days exploring Split, the jewel of the Adriatic. The narrow streets with steep steps, led to tower like structures. The very ornate buildings were the remains and reminders of the Roman Emperor, Diocletian.

We saw beautiful plazas, which were lined with tables and coffee drinking visitors. It didn't even feel like we were in the war, except for the shortage of food and goods. There

were carabiniere patrolling the streets, but they were very benevolent. They talked to everyone and even shared some chocolates with the kids in the neighborhood. The Italian fascists wore black shirts and marching boots as well, but in their chests beat a human heart.

The cobblestone streets, with their narrow sidewalks, all seemed to lead to the waterfront, where they embraced the beautiful blue Adriatic as it splashed and caressed them. We often walked to the waterfront where we watched small sailboats in many different colors.

In Split we found some old friends of my parents, who were still operating a shoe store. This place became a meeting place for the few Jews who escaped from Serbia and the Nazis. The shoe store became a message center for those who lost relatives and were trying to find them. The shoe store became a grieving place, the place where many refugees cried hysterically and emotionally and said goodbye to their massacred families.

The atrocities of the war were raging only a few miles away, but in Split the sun was shining. And we knew that the Nazis were only a few steps away from us.

A few days later, Aunt Erna and Uncle Ralph came to Split. They also learned about the shoe store and inquired about our whereabouts. We connected with them and found another apartment that accommodated both families. I was happy in our new apartment, but I wanted to know what happened to the lady with the negligée. My father would never talk about it.

My dad and my uncle immediately started making cookies again. The flour, eggs and sugar were only available on the black market. My aunt and my mother would sneak some flour, and make small buns for me and Ike. We handled the bread like a national treasure every time we went to the beach to go swimming in the Adriatic. The water was unbelievably clean, blue and translucent.

One day, while on the beach, I stepped on some cut glass and cut the soles of both my feet. I ran to the lifeguard, who poured some awful burning solution on my feet, and I had to sit there crying and wait for my parents to pick us up. The wounds on both my feet got infected, and there was no cream or medication that would clear up the infection. My mother took me to a few doctors, but they came up with nothing. One doctor even said that it might be some kind of venereal disease.

"What is venereal disease?" I wanted to know. To which my mother didn't even bother to answer.

Another doctor said, that if the infection did not clear up, I might lose both my feet. Of course, I became hysterical. When we got home, a neighbor came over to see why I was crying so loud.

"I thought you were killing her," the neighbor said. She looked at my feet, and said, "Is that all? I have just the thing to heal your feet." A few minutes later, she came back with two halves of tomatoes.

"I put my magic potion on these tomatoes. They will heal you fast."

My mother put the tomatoes on the soles of my feet, put bandages over them, and started to say something negative, when my father interrupted her, and said to the neighbor, "Thank you. I know your magic will work." He winked at me, like he believed her.

I looked at my dad. He never lied to me, and if he thought her magic would work, I believed her, also. My mother

washed and kissed my feet, and changed the tomatoes every day, for about three days, when she realized that the wounds on both feet were turning pale pink, and the infection was fading. To this day, I don't know what healed me, her magic, my mind, my mother's kisses, or the tomatoes. I really didn't care about being philosophical. I just didn't want to lose my feet.

One day, as my aunt was delivering the cookies, a carabiniere stopped her, and wanted to see what was in the box.

"Just an empty box," she said shaking.

He let her go, but from that day on, they found a large doll box with a doll picture on it, and I started delivering all the cookies. My uncle showed me how to hop and skip, while I carried the doll box with my father or my uncle walking behind me. I delivered the cookies and I was never stopped. At a young age, I started learning how to make money.

I also wanted to help with the cookies, so my uncle showed me how to break the eggs. One day I broke an egg that had a very foul odor. I threw it on the floor, and watched the yellow splash all over, spreading the atrocious smell.

"What did you do?" my uncle screamed at me.

"I threw the rotten egg away," I said, in tears. I was not used to them ever getting angry with me.

Both my parents came in the kitchen and wanted to know what I did. My uncle showed them the egg, which had splashed all over the floor and the wall.

"What is that terrible smell?" my mother asked.

"Eggs," my uncle said. "They sold us rotten eggs."

"We'll just have to use extra vanilla," my aunt laughed out loud.

We all laughed, while my uncle doubled up on the vanilla. The cookies had a little different taste, but one would never think it was rotten eggs. We remembered the story of the rotten eggs for a long time afterward.

One day, a neighbor came in drawn by the delicious smell of baking cookies. She wanted to know where we bought the ingredients. My aunt wanted to help her out, so she told her about the black market. A few hours later, carabiniere came in, went directly to where the sugar and flower were stored, collected all the ingredients, and arrested my uncle and my father for black marketing.

Even though I knew that the Italians were not as hard and as bad as the Nazis, I didn't like my father and my uncle being taken away to jail.

While they were incarcerated, my mother and my aunt ran all over the city trying to get them out. In the meantime, we were able to visit them, take them food and clean clothing.

My aunt and my mother continued making cookies, while I happily delivered them. I just knew that I had to be home at a certain time because of the curfew.

Nothing significant happened to us in Split during the next few months.

However, in July of 1942, Hitler ordered the deportation of the rest of the Jews, from Poland and Belgium, to Auschwitz. Around the same time, Treblinka extermination camp was established in Poland, near Warsaw. It contained 10 gas chambers, where the Jews were told to take a shower, but instead of water, they were doused with carbon monoxide. After they were dead, the Nazis burned their bodies in open pits. They did not want to bury them because of fear of contaminating the drinking water.

At the end of six months, my uncle and my father were released from the Italian jail. My mother was so happy to see my dad, that she got pregnant against her wishes. She was happy that my dad was out and alive, but she did not want a newborn child in such difficult times. She would have had an abortion but those were not available in Italy. She tried drinking different solutions in order to abort, but to no avail. The fetus survived, and she was to have another son.

Around the middle of 1943, Italy signed a pact with the Allies. And, we knew we had to make tracks again. We were still in Split, when Germany, angered by the Italian action, started bombing Split. Once again, we found ourselves being attacked by German aircraft. I was so scared. "Are they going to get us this time?" I wondered.

One night, we heard the sirens warning us of bombing. But this time the sound of aircraft was different. It sounded full and heavy. We ran to our favorite cave, overlooking the Adriatic sea. There were many people there already. My brother, Ike, and I were the smallest, so they pushed us all the way inside the cave, to the point where the ceiling met the floor, at an angle.

"These are not German planes," someone whispered.

"They are American!" someone else exclaimed.

"They are going to save us!" a woman screeched.

"Are you stupid?" a man's voice echoed, in back of the cave. "They are here to bomb us! These are the flying fortresses, and they are here to bomb us!"

When I heard the flying fortresses, I envisioned a castle, like the one where Rapunzel lowered her hair, and waited for her lover to climb up to her.

The Flying Fortress, the B17 aircraft flew over our cave, with a thundering sound, but did not choose to bomb us. This time we were lucky.

Early the next morning, we heard the sirens again and we ran to our cave. It was under the mountain, Marjan. As before, Ike and I were pushed all the way in, and then the adults piled in. The ceiling was low, and it was hard to breath. There was a lot of dust, and we were choking and coughing. Then we heard and felt the fury of the German planes. They flew low over our mountain, aimed and dropped one bomb after another, trying to kill everything in sight, especially in the cave.

A bomb hit the mountain. We shook. The gravel and rocks dislodged from the impact of the mountain, burying everything inside. The planes circled over the mountain again and again, enjoying the results of their evil acts. When the planes left, the adults rolled out of the cave. One by one they exited the cave, dusting off their clothes and taking deep

breaths of air.

When my parents got out, they looked for me and Ike. We were nowhere to be seen. In a state of panic, my father crawled back into the cave and with his bare hands started to dig his children out from under the powdery rocks.

When they dug us out, we were so scared that neither of us said a word. We gasped for air, and held on to our parents. While I was buried under the rocks, I thought that they would never find me, and that I was going to die of suffocation inside that cave. I was buried alive, but God must have been there with me because here I am, alive, telling the story.

My uncle, trying to get out from the cave, had a sharp rock puncture his back, and he suffered with it for the rest of his life.

In the next few days we heard the German tanks and artillery coming close to Split. We had no choice. We had to leave, but we didn't know how, or where. Once again, my parents resorted to the little gold pouch tucked into my mother's bosom. There were only two rings left.

We packed in a hurry, and only took a few things. The six of us went to the port, hoping to get a boat to take us across the Adriatic, to Italy. It seemed like half the town was trying to get into one small boat. The captain stood at the edge of his boat, hitting everyone with an iron bar, deterring them from climbing on board.

As before, my mother took out one of the rings and showed it to the captain. He started to hit her. Then he noticed the

ring. He grabbed it, and motioned to us to get in the boat. A few minutes later, we felt the gentle waves of the beautiful Adriatic.

In a few hours, we saw the Island of Korchula, which was half way between Yugoslavia and Bari, Italy. The captain got off the boat and tied it to the dock. As we disembarked, we realized that the whole island smelled of fish and wine. We were hungry, tired and cold, and the fish smelled delicious. My aunt and uncle were singing. They said that the smell of wine was making them drunk.

In September of 1943, the Germans occupied Rome and Northern Italy. In their desperation for the final solution, the Nazis started collecting Jews from all over Italy. No one could explain to me, the passion Germans had for the elimination of all the Jews.

Once again, we were a few steps away from death. On the island, we found a room, and my father did odd jobs to keep us going. We ate a lot of fish and smelled like everyone else on the island. But, that too, was not to last. We heard German guns and aircraft, and we knew they had entered Split.

By now the British occupied Bari, Italy, and we knew this was our next destination. Again, we packed our few rags, and the six of us went to the marina, hoping to get another boat to take us across the Adriatic, to Italy.

Bari,

Italia

Chapter 9

BARI, ITALIA

In September of 1943, Italy capitulated, and allied forces entered Bari, Italy. When we got there, it was already buzzing with beautiful young men in uniform, with Royal Air Force insignias. The British were aware of all the refugees that poured into Bari, so they opened a school, threw straw on the cold marbled floors, and allowed us to spend a few nights there.

During the few days we spent at the school, we watched many more refugees arrive in Bari. Many of them were Jews from all over Europe. And some of those were people my parents knew from Yugoslavia.

A young boy, in particular, caught my eye and I experienced the same feeling as I did when I watched the prostitute and the Italian general, through my window in Split. I was fourteen years old and the woman in me had started to awaken.

The British soldiers gave us bread, chocolates and tea with milk. I always drank tea with lemon, so this was a new experience for me.

We stayed at the school for a few days. Then, we started looking for a place to live. We joined with some other people and rented a villa in a small town of Carbonara, a few miles outside of Bari. The villa had all marbled floors and no heat. The Joint Distribution Committee helped us with rent, but there was hardly any money for food, or anything else.

My mother was a few months pregnant, and there was no nutrition or vitamins, or even food for her. I watched her often bend over the toilet and throw up the little food she had eaten. I felt bad for her. She was still young, but her youth seemed to have been stolen from her by the war. We were all in the same place, but she seemed to take it the hardest.

On December 2nd, 1943, she started to bleed so we rushed her to the hospital in Bari. The hospital was close to the port, and I remember looking at the ships from the hospital window. At 7:25 that evening, suddenly, there appeared out of nowhere, a lot of airplanes throwing flares, and lighting up the skies and the port. It looked like daylight, but it was German planes attacking the British navy and a few American ships, in the port of Bari.

The bombs exploded over the entire port. Explosion, detonation, devastation and death were everywhere. In my mind it was 1941 again, when Germany first bombed Yugoslavia. There was no place to run or hide. Everyone stood frozen in time and space. I held onto the railing of the brown metal bed with both hands. There was chaos everywhere. Screams and cries and dust filled the hospital.

Then, the light faded and the bombing stopped for a few minutes, but then it resumed with a vengeance. I prayed that it would stop while we are still alive. Bari was on fire. The

bombing was so vicious and severe, that it became known as the little Pearl Harbor. Part of the hospital was destroyed, but the maternity ward remained intact.

Seventeen British cargo ships were sunk during the raid, which lasted for over an hour. Some of the German planes came from Italian airports, and some from Yugoslavian. This was meant to be a surprise attack by the Germans, and it was. Among the sunken vessels, was the U.S.S. Liberty, and the John Harvey. Unfortunately, the John Harvey carried 2,000 tons of sulphur mustard, which they kept in case Germany resorted to germ warfare. However, when the bombs hit the vessel, the gas spilled and mixed with oil, which escaped from the vessels, thus causing many severe burns to the sailors who had jumped into the water to escape the explosion. The allies and Winston Churchill declared that the burns were caused by enemy actions. Later on, Dwight D. Eisenhower approved the report.

Once more, we were protected by His Grace. It was like God had put His curtain of light around us and protected us from all evil.

A few days later we went back to our villa in Carbonara. Shortly after that, I met and befriended an Italian girl, who took me home to meet her family. Her father's name was Pastore Donato. I thought that his name was as beautiful as the whole family. There were eight children, who were all adored by their parents. In the backyard they had a lovely stone sanctuary, with the Madonna holding her child. They were very religious, and truly lived it.

When I told them that my mother was expecting a baby, they took a big box, filled it with food and lots of baby clothes,

and took it to her. It was amazing. There were hand knitted sweaters, diapers, lace tops and many blankets. I am sure they suspected that we were Jewish, but never asked any questions.

Each of the kids had a bicycle and they wanted to teach me how to ride. Even though I was scared, it was not in my nature to back off. I got on and fell off. I got on again, and went back and forth, and then fell. I got on again and stayed on. We rode on the main street of Bari. It was muddy and wet. The traffic was horrendous. There were army trucks, tanks, cars, and horse and buggy carriages. I panicked. I could hardly see in front of me, so I closed my eyes and fell in the puddle of mud, in front of a huge army truck full of soldiers. I heard the brakes screech. I heard the soldiers laugh, but I still kept my eyes closed. A few minutes later, in what seemed like a week, I felt arms pulling me out of the mud. I got up, got back on the bicycle, and we proceeded home.

My accident, however couldn't even come close to the situation that occurred in Europe, at the same time. In the death camp of Sobibar, 300 Soviet POWs and Jews attempted an escape. As they tried to run out of the gate, the Nazis opened fire with their machine guns and massacred most of the prisoners. The 300 escaped, and out of 300, only fifty survived. After that episode, the Nazis exterminated the rest of 250,000 people in that camp, and closed it. They destroyed the camp and planted trees, in order to conceal any and all traces of the atrocities which they committed there.

When I returned home to our villa all muddy, after the bicycle episode, my mother gave me clean clothes and of course, scolded me for being careless. After I changed, I

realized that everyone in the house was busy cleaning the house, and cooking the little food we had. The other families, living with us, were setting the table, sweeping the floors and making everything pretty.

"We are going to have company for dinner," my mother told me.

"Who? Who is coming?" I was excited.

At about 5 P.M., four American sailors came to our house for dinner. They each brought a bag full of food. There was bread, chocolates, cans of beans, and chewing gum. Lots of chewing gum. I had never seen chewing gum before. I took a Chicklet with delight, tasted its delicious flavor, chewed it, and then swallowed it, making a weird sound.

"You are not supposed to swallow it," they laughed. "You chew it, then pull it," and all of them pulled the gum in long strands, and then put it back into their mouths. So of course, I had to try again. I put another piece of gum in my mouth, chewed it, and started pulling it. But for some reason, my gum stuck to my fingers, then to my hands, then I had gum everywhere. By now, everyone was laughing. For a moment I felt uncomfortable, but then, I, too, burst out laughing. I liked laughing with them. We all had such a good time.

First, we all had homemade bread, with heavy, local olive oil and garlic. The second course was a vegetarian soup with lots of celery and carrots. Everyone slurped it with delight. Then we had broccolini. I had never had broccolini before.

In between courses, the sailors told us many stories about America. I loved to hear about America. It always reminded

me of Shirley Temple and her tap dancing. When the main course came to the table, the sailors looked puzzled. This was a delicacy, and besides, it was the only protein we could get.

"Smells delicious. What is it?" one of the sailors inquired.

No one answered.

"Tastes good, but different," another sailor said.

"It's fried brains," I said, very loudly, in my soprano voice.

The sailors opened their eyes wide, ran to the bathroom, and a few minutes later, we could hear the engine of their jeep. I felt bad, because I didn't even get to say goodby to them. *I wondered if they thought those were human brains?*

One morning, I woke up, and I had a rash all over my body. I was itching, scratching and bleeding all over, as was my brother, Ike. My parents didn't know what to do with us. We had no medication or money. Someone suggested that my parents take us to a Catholic convent, and let the nuns take care of us. We knew that the nuns were instrumental many times during the war, in saving Jews, particularly children.

We went into town, found the convent, and knocked on the heavy tall, dark doors that reminded me of a dungeon. Two sisters wearing black habits and white head wear, came out and looked at us. Both Ike and I were covered with bloody sores. The sisters said nothing, but extended their arms, motioning me and Ike to go in. They smiled and took us in, closing the heavy doors behind us.

With tears in their eyes, my parents released us, not knowing if they were ever going to see us again. It was a time when the world had turned upside down. It was a time when friend went against friend. It was a time when no-one trusted anyone. It was a time when one's own shadow was frightening. It was a time when the world had disconnected from God.

Two nuns took me and Ike into a large room with tall columns and cold marble floors. One of the nuns brought an aluminum tub, like the one we used to do our laundry in. The nuns tore off our clothes and threw them against the wall. Then they told me and Ike to step into the tub. We were naked, vulnerable and cold. The room echoed with every step and every sound. *What are they going to do to us?* I panicked. Both Ike and I were shaking with cold and fear. They could see that Ike was circumcised, but said nothing. One of the nuns brought a pitcher of hot water and poured it in the bucket. *Were they going to cook us like Hansel and Gretel?*

Their black habits swished, as they walked. Another nun took a hard brush and started scrubbing our limp bodies, until she drew blood. I looked at the water in the bucket, which turned redder and redder, with our blood. Horrible thoughts came to my mind. For a moment, I even thought that they wanted to bleed us to death. I was scared. And Ike, who was 9 years old, was dumb with fear. He didn't even cry. He held on to my hand tightly.

The nuns scrubbed our bodies until every scab was gone. They put a gentle cream on us. They then wrapped us in soft towels and gave us fresh clothes. This was followed with delicious bread and olive oil with garlic.

"This will keep the bugs off you," one of the nuns said smiling.

We had to pray every day we were at the convent. A few days later, my parents picked us up and took us home, completely healed.

Those Italian Nuns were a true expression of God's love.

After a while, it seemed that our lives were settled, and we just waited for the war to be over, so we could return home to Yugoslavia. In the meantime, my father started a vegetable garden in the back yard of the villa. I loved helping him plant onions and garlic and work the soil.

One morning, in March, 1943, I got up and went outside as usual. I couldn't believe what I saw. The air was red, and impregnated with particles of smoke, soot and dust. It seemed that the entire earth was enveloped with a red curtain. The foul odor of sulphur penetrated my nose and my eyes. It was impossible to breath. It was the volcano at Mount Vesuvius near Napoli, waking itself and everyone else within miles and miles around.

The last time it had awakened, was in 79 AD, when thousands of people perished. I remembered studying about Pompey in school, and its devastation. The only difference was, that at that time, people thought it was Gods doing the destroying.

I, of course, knew about Vesuvius. Both times, curtains of smoke enveloped the countryside. The lava, which escaped from the crater, came flowing down 30 to 90 feet high, consuming everything in its path. The temperature near the

lava rose to about 2,000 F. Surrounding villages were covered with many feet of ash. The smoke seemed to linger for weeks, but then it cleared, and all was back to normal.

One of the ladies who shared our villa worked for the British forces. She was the supervisor in an alterations department, and she asked my parents if I could go with her and help her in the sewing room. My parents consented. And I started shortening the soldier's pants and shirt sleeves, and sewing on buttons. That is when I learned to sew and flirt, even though I never got near any soldiers. I even got paid for that.

Every Friday, when the soldiers got their rations, I too got my brown paper bag full of goodies as well. It was such a joy for me to take the bag home to my parents and Ike. I loved to watch them open the bag, and examine each item of food with joy and savor. I was only fourteen years old, but I felt like a bread earner. I loved the feeling of giving love back to my parents. For me, bread and chocolates were the most important.

The Germans knew that the war was nearing an end, so with an insane fury they dug in and collected the rest of the Jews from Hungary, raided a school in France because they hid some Jewish children, and collected the rest of the Jews from Vienna, and sent all of them to Auschwitz. It was extermination to the end.

In November of 1943, the U.S. Congress held hearings about the State Department's inaction concerning the massacre of the European Jews. And, in January of 1944, Roosevelt under political pressure, created a War Refugee Board. The board eventually saved about 200,000 Jews from death and concentration camps. However, the board did not accomplish

its full capacity, because of the disabling circumstances of the United States Government.

In March of 1944, another event almost took place. A German officer, Eberhard von Breitenbuch foreseeing the end of the war and total destruction of Germany, wanted to stop Hitler from going any further.

He hid a small pistol in his pocket, even though he knew it would cost him his life. He wanted to assassinate Hitler. He, however, was stopped, and his plan never went into effect.

In 1939, Johann George Eiser, who did not like Nazi control of the unions and religious restrictions, got a bomb which was to explode during Hitler's speech in the Burgenbrau Beer Cellar in Munich. For some reason, Hitler left a few minutes early. He missed the bomb, which exploded and killed a few people, and wounded many.

There were a few other plans for assassination, but for some reason, they, too, were aborted, or simply failed.

In the meantime, a young reporter for the New York Herald Tribune, Dr. Ruth Gruber, wanted to do something about the terrible Jewish situation in Europe. She went to Washington and knocked on many different doors, until she finally connected with President Roosevelt's Secretary of the Interior, Harold Ickes. Through Dr. Ruth Gruber's efforts, and other political pressures, President Roosevelt consented to bring 1,000 refugees from war torn Europe to the united States, as his guests.

We were still living at the villa in Carbonara when the news about the 1,000 refugees reached us. My parents and my aunt

and uncle went to Bari immediately to find out who could qualify. We were told that families with small children, and in good health, were good candidates. My little brother, Michael was only a few months old, so our chances of being selected were very good.

To reinforce our chances for qualification, we entered into a displaced persons camp that was run by the British. There we could keep track of what was going on and how the selection was taking place. Again, we packed our few rags and left the villa to the people who were sharing it with us. I hated leaving the villa. I had beautiful memories of me and Aunt Erna eating bread, and olive oil with garlic, and singing Italian songs in harmony. I also loved my job at the British Royal Air force sewing room.

The DP camp was nothing like the Nazi death camps, but it was pretty grim. I remember the communal tent showers. It was the first time I saw women's breasts hang like flaps of skin, and their rib cages protruding like they were going to come right out of their skin. Some women had lost most of their hair, so from the back, I couldn't tell if they were women or men.

There, we were given a small quantity of mediocre food, but we were not starving. We were in the camp for a few weeks before the selection began. I was nervous and I was scared. America was all the way at the other end of the world, and I did not speak "American" language. We all held our breath.

"There are thousands and thousands of refugees," my mother despaired. "Why would they choose us? There are people who are much worse off than we are. We'll never be selected."

"Don't you worry your little head," my father smiled. "We made it so far, didn't we?"

There were refugees who had been in concentration camps. There were elderly people, who cried and begged to be allowed to spend the rest of their lives in peace in America.

It looked like the people who were doing the selection were playing God, but I am sure that their job was not easy. *How do you choose from thousands of broken spirits and broken bodies? How do you decide who is to go to safety, and who is to remain in Hell?*

Finally, in the middle of all that chaos, the news spread. The Danons were selected to go to America. My aunt and my uncle were singing and dancing with joy, while my mother couldn't stop mourning for her father and all her sisters and brothers who were massacred by the Nazis. Her pain was so great that her whole life became meaningless and without joy.

In the early morning, we, the selected one thousand were loaded into trucks and driven to Naples, where we were to board a ship to America.

The Henry Gibbins was a Red Cross ship which took wounded soldiers back home. It also took us, the refugees, to freedom. The Henry Gibbins was one of the 29 ships in the flotilla going to the United States. Some of the ships in the flotilla brought back 100,000 German prisoners of war, who were going to be in a prisoner of war camp until the war ended. At the end of the war, they were to be shipped back.

And so it was, in August of 1944, that we left Italy and the

terror of the war, and we were on our way to America. We were invited to be the guests of President Roosevelt. It was a dream come true, and I was afraid of waking up. I couldn't get too exited, however, about our new lives because I hated the ocean, and I knew I would get seasick. And besides, we still had to cross the Atlantic ocean, and leave ourselves vulnerable to German aircraft and an ocean full of mines.

The Henry Gibbins

Chapter 10

THE HENRY GIBBINS

In my mind, we were the guests of President Roosevelt, and that was exciting. I thought our accommodations were going to be very nice. After all, he was the President of America. Everything in America is beautiful.

We, all of us refugees, started climbing aboard the ship.

"We are actually going to America," my uncle sang.

But in spite of our joy, we sure painted a sad picture. Thin. Pale. Dressed in rags. Shoes stuffed with newspapers to cover the holes. Dirty hair, broken spirits. Some carrying suitcases, some paper bags, and some just a bundle of rags.

As we were shown our accommodations, I panicked. I realized that we were being taken to a lower deck, where there were no windows or air. The area was dim and very stuffy. I could hardly breathe. It was like going into the cave again to be buried alive. And then the horror struck me. The entire area was lined with denim bunks, which were many deep. People, one on top of the other, with only two feet in between them. It was pretty awful. Nor, was it worthy of the

President's guests.

At 15, I needed and wanted some privacy. My breasts were starting to form. I wasn't about to dress or undress in front of a thousand people. The bunks were lined up on top of each other, so close that I could hear people below me, above me, and around me, breathe, snore and fart. The showers were also communal. I found that devastating, but there was no choice. Eventually, I started to appreciate and enjoy the warm water which caressed my body. There was also soap, which we had not had for a while.

Since many of us came from different countries, like Yugoslavia, Germany, Poland, Austria and many others, there were many different languages spoken and many different cultures exhibited. Our ship, the Henry Gibbins became like a little Europe. Not only did we all speak different languages, but many times there were misunderstandings and even fights among the refugees due to misunderstandings and class distinctions.

Even the kids were divided into groups. There were the older kids of seventeen and eighteen. There were we, fourteen to sixteen, and then there were little kids. It was a microcosm of the world. There were those of very high education and there were some just common, nice people like my family. The German Jews thought they were too good for the rest of us.

There were Sephardic Jews, who were descendants from Spain, and Ashkenazi Jews who came from Eastern Europe. It was truly a melting pot, with only one thing in common: we all had survived the Nazi atrocities.

There was, however, one saving grace; food. There was a lot of food. It was served two times a day. Breakfast and dinner. When we all got in line in the cafeteria, I looked at all the food in disbelief. It was the first time I saw canned beans. They were sweet, gooey and delicious. I ate so fast that the brown, syrupy sauce covered not only my mouth, but my face as well. A lady in a nurse's uniform, whom I had not seen before, came towards me smiling.

"You don't have to eat so fast. There is plenty of food for all, and more than enough to fill you up." she said, as she took a towel and wiped off my face. "Eat slower, it will feel better," and then she was lost in the crowded cafeteria.

Everyone was standing and stuffing their faces because the cafeteria was set up for standing only. We all looked like chipmunks, with our cheeks extended with the huge amounts of food we stuffed in our mouths.

There was white bread like I had never seen before. It was soft and sweet and delicious. It wrapped itself over my tongue and my teeth and it made my stomach smile. I had to try everything. I ate until I thought I was going to explode. I was trying to make up for the four years of starving.

No sooner did I swallow my last bite than I felt the ship swaying from side to side. My meal did not sit very well. Suddenly, it all started to come back. I put my hand over my mouth, trying to hold it back until I found a bathroom. I barely made it over the toilet, as I felt and watched all that beautiful food saying goodby to me. From then on, I ate smaller quantities, but my stomach refused to keep anything down. The only time I felt comfortable, and not seasick, was when I was outside on the deck, lying down and looking up

at the sky.

The deck was where most of the activities took place. Every morning we had English lessons from Dr. Ruth Gruber. Up to that time, I had never met Dr. Gruber. There she stood in front of a black board. She was petite, blonde and gorgeous. At first I though she was a movie star. And then I realized who she was. She was the one who went to Europe, in the middle of Hell, and risked her own life to save ours. She was just as beautiful inside as she was outside.

Besides English lessons, there was a nurse and a medic on the deck. They set up a station where they dispensed medications. It seemed that every day they gave us shots for something else. There were also lines for candies, particularly life savers and gum. I hated shots and usually hid when they were being doled out.

One time, there was a long line. I asked what it was for. I was told that they were giving us not only lifesavers, but chocolates as well. I was not about to miss the chocolates. I got in line and chatted in Italian with the girl in front of me. Since we all lived in Italy during hiding, Italian became our Esperanto, our own common language. The girl in front of me was from Hungary, and she was there with her two sisters and her parents. They were lucky as well to get out of that hell all together.

When I came to the end of the line, I recognized the nurses who previously gave me shots. A hand grabbed me by the arm and gave me a shot. I protested, but they just stuck a roll of lifesavers in my hand and pushed me away from the line. I never got into another line again.

In the mornings, we also had safety drills. The sirens cried out. We all had to go to the main deck, put on the lifesaver vests and stand in line.

One evening, after we had all gone to bed, we heard the wailing sound of the sirens. I knew that this was for real and not a drill. Everyone started to stir, cry and pray in confusion. We were instructed to put on our vests and remain quiet and stay on our denim cots. No one moved. We were all paralyzed with fear. Even my little brother Michael, who was only five months old, was quiet. He was the best baby I ever saw. He never cried and he smiled a lot.

Being bombed on the land was bad, but on the ship there was no place to run and hide. Had we been bombed on the ship, we would have sunk, and all drowned.

There were 12 German war planes circling our fleet. We heard our anti-aircraft guns and hoped that they wouldn't miss. A heavy smoke filled our entire floor. It seemed that someone forgot to close the chute to our floor allowing the smoke to penetrate our quarters and envelop all the refugees.

I thought we were going to suffocate. There was no oxygen. We were all coughing and choking. There was not only smoke, but also the smell of ammunition. One of the ships in the convoy had released this heavy smoke, attempting to hide the Red Cross ship with wounded American soldiers and refugees. It must have worked, because the German planes left without hurting us.

I thought that they did not hurt us because of the hundred thousand German prisoners of war. One more time, we were

saved by a miracle.

Amongst the refugees, we had several people with heavenly voices. They sang to us and made us happy. They also had a show for the wounded Americans. The group consisted of a fabulous tenor, an opera star from Zagreb, Yugoslavia.

One of my favorite arias he sang, was *"Figaro" from "Barber of Seville."* There were a few sopranos, an accordion player and a few girls who could sing in different languages. The girls were very beautiful, which drove the American soldiers crazy. One girl in particular stood out. She had a beautiful figure, flowing blonde hair and a voice like Marlene Dietrich. She always wore an army uniform, which made her look like an ad for the army recruiting office. I am ashamed to admit, but I was jealous of the beautiful girls. I never thought of myself as beautiful or smart.

Many of the wounded soldiers whistled at our girls and yelled, "Marry me, doll. I love you!"

At 15, I was just a little, inexperienced, uneducated kid who nobody looked at. The war had robbed me of 4 years of life, education and youth experiences. Many of the refugee kids already spoke English, which made me feel even more dumb and more invisible. I knew I had it in me to be smart, but life had dealt me a rotten hand and I had to play it the best I could.

The trip to America lasted 13 days, which for me were mostly spent eating and throwing up. The 13 days felt like a year. I remembered the days we spent in our house in Belgrade during Nazi occupation, with all those people who were joking about going to America. And now we were

really on our way there. It was not a dream or a fantasy, it was real.

It was August, and it was warm and humid, when we approached New York Harbor. We were all hanging around the rails of the ship's deck, holding our breath with excitement, when we saw her. The lady with the draped robe, holding the lit torch in her hand. She stood there, tall, proud, welcoming us with love. The Statue of Liberty. Everyone on the deck cried. Many kissed the steel floor of the ship, after all, it was the ground of the United States of America.

> *Not like the brazen giant of Greek fame,*
> *With conquering limbs astride from land to land;*
> *Here at our sea-washed, sunset gates shall stand*
> *A mighty woman with a torch, whose flame*
> *Is the imprisoned lightning, and her name*
> *Mother of Exiles. From her beacon-hand*
> *Glows world-wide welcome; her mild eyes command*
> *The air-bridged harbor that twin cities frame.*
> *"Keep ancient lands, your storied pomp," cries she,*
> *With silent lips.* **Give me your tired, your poor,**
> **Your huddled masses yearning to breathe free,**
> **The wretched refuse of your teeming shore.**
> **Send these, the homeless, tempest-tossed to me,**
> **I lift my lamp beside the golden door.**
> *Emma Lazarus, 1883*

This was the poem inscribed on the stand where she proudly stood. Those words were especially meaningful to us refugees, because it was Emma Lazarus, a Jewish Poetess, who wrote them, many years ago.

We came with love for this land. We came with pride. We came eager to learn, absorb and give back We came with gratitude, not with entitlement.

Yes, we were tired, and we were poor, but now we were in America. And in America, everyone is rich. My father used to tell me how in America, people are free to work at whatever they want, and for as long they wish. He reminded me, that in Yugoslavia he had to close the store between 12:00 and 3:00, and go home and have lunch. The cops would patrol the streets, and if someone was open, they would get a ticket.

My father also told me that in America, you can practice your own religion and no one bothers you. You could even say what you feel without being shot. I loved America from the beginning, even though I did not fully understand what all the freedoms were or what they meant.

My father was excited. He was not afraid of work, as long as he was allowed to do it. Even my mother, who was depressed most of the time, had a smile on her face.

"Maybe we can have a good life again," she cried. "But my family, they can't have any life at all."

My father comforted her, as he put his arms around her and my baby brother, Michael.

"This is a new beginning for us, so let's give thanks to God for our lives."

My mother wiped off her tears and gave another feeble smile

Many of the refugees cried with joy, and others had their eyes closed reciting silent prayers of gratitude.

Shortly after we dropped anchor in New York, we all stood at the ship's railing watching the skyscrapers and other tall buildings. To me it felt like I was watching a movie because I had never seen such tall buildings. I could also see the activities that were taking place on land below. There were many army trucks, fire engines and many ambulances. Hundreds of people were hurrying back and forth. There was a band playing some marching music. When the ship totally stopped, the M. P.'s dropped a plank from the ship to land, and we watched as the wounded soldiers started exiting the ship. Some were in wheelchairs, some on crutches and some on stretchers. They were all waiving to us while we waved goodbye to them.

They were home, but where are we going? I thought. *Where is going to be our new home?* I was excited with the prospect of going back to school, until I remembered that I did not speak the language. Panic filled me again, but all the noise and all the distractions would not allow me to stay in that place.

We stayed on the ship one more day. When we finally got off the ship, we were herded to a building which may have been a hospital at one time. The men were separated from the women and children. A hysterical panic enveloped all the refugees. That was the first thing the Nazis did in the concentration camps. They separated the men from the women, and then shot them.

"Are the Americans going to kill us also? Why are they separating us. What is going on?" These were some of the

questions the refugees uttered.

Ruth Gruber had gone home to Brooklyn, so there was no one to answer our questions and ease our panic. After a while, we were ordered to undress and put all our clothes in a knit bag, and close it by pulling the strings. Some people even thought the soldiers were going to turn on the gas, like the Nazis did in the showers of the concentration camps.

We held on to each other. Our bodies were naked, pale and skeletal, and shaking with fear. Some soldiers came in with sprayers, wearing masks. They sprayed us all over, especially the hair, under arms and the pubic areas. Then we realized that they were disinfecting us, by killing all the lice that might have come for a free ride. When they finished spraying us they gave us back our clothes. However, the clothes had been disinfected as well. They must have run our clothes through a steamer because when we put them on, they were terribly wrinkled, shrunken and ruined.

Shortly after, Ruth Gruber returned and informed us of our destination. Our new home was to be an old army camp which was turned into apartments, so that the family units could stay together and have some privacy.

The army camp was the old Fort Ontario, in Oswego, New York, on Lake Ontario. To me, that didn't mean anything. I didn't know where Fort Ontario was. And I didn't care. I was tired and hungry. We were all tired. We just wanted to settle somewhere and put our heads on pillows. My brother Ike was tired and cranky, especially since he was replaced with Michael. My mother couldn't give Ike all the attention she did before because she had to share it with Michael. My baby brother, Michael, was his wonderful self, and just

smiled at everyone who came near him.

If we didn't look like refugees before, we sure did now. We had hardly any other clothes and not much of anything else. This made it very easy for us to move from one to place to another. A few people, however had a few suitcases each. They were able to even save the candelabra for Shabat, (Friday evening services and prayers.)

To get to Oswego, we had to take a train. Another trip which seemed eternal.

Fort

Ontario

Chapter 11

FORT ONTARIO

The train stopped. And we were escorted to the fort. The first thing we saw was a chain link fence with barbed wires on top. In our minds it was a concentration camp all over again. There were people who refused to enter and had to be subdued by the guards. Others were crying and protesting.

"Is this a joke?" an intellectual, from Yugoslavia, yelled out.

"I thought we were the personal guests of President Roosevelt. What are you doing to us?"

My mother was holding Michael, while Ike and I held on to my father for wisdom.

"We are in America. We are free. Don't worry about a little fence." My dad winked at my mother. "Things are never what they seem."

I often wondered about my dad. Was he never afraid, or did he fake it to make us feel better. But, whatever it was, it was O.K. His positive attitude always put us at ease, and I knew that it was his positive thinking that brought us through the

war and into safety.

We entered the Refugee Emergency Shelter at Fort Ontario, with its huge grassy fields, white barracks and other brick buildings. As we approached our barrack, we walked up the stairs and realized that our names were on the door of one of the apartments. The agency had given each family a small apartment, which was converted just for us. There were cots, tables, chairs and lockers. We had pillows and sheets and blankets. I felt that this was the height of luxury.

But no matter how great it was, I would wake up at night crying in fear. Many times my mom or my dad would sit on the edge of my bed, and hold me, and remind me that we were in America. I got especially frightened when an airplane flew low over our heads. The fear of airplanes dropping bombs on us did not leave me for many years to come.

Shortly after, the sun came up bringing a new day and new life, which was exciting. I couldn't wait to explore and find out who else lived in our barrack. I was so hoping it would be Koki, the boy who I saw in Bari while we were at the school sitting on the floor in the straw.

Barracks at Fort Ontario.

Each barrack had four open showers, with bathrooms. The upper ones were for women and the lower for men.

Besides our living quarters, there were other buildings. A brick building for administrative purposes, a recreation room, and a barrack which was converted into a sanctuary. There were also barracks which served as mess halls. Because there were so many different nationalities, there were a few different dining rooms.

There was a lot of food, milk and juices. What fascinated me the most were the cornflakes boxes, which we cut in the

middle and poured milk into them, and ate right out of the box. No dishes to wash.

The Americans are very smart, I thought.

Everyone filled their purses, pockets and bags with food from the dining room, which they took to their own little dens.

My father and my aunt Erna ran our Sephardic kitchen. My uncle baked the most wonderful tortas and cookies and pastries. Many people would come to our dining room, after they had dinner in their own, just for desert. My aunt Erna did not spare herself. She created the most gourmet meals ever. My father recruited men and women to help clean and maintain our kitchen.

The first Sunday at the fort was celebrated with speeches given by different dignitaries from the State Department, City of Oswego, a minister and a rabbi. They welcomed us to their beautiful town of Oswego.

People from our group stood up and in their broken English, said, "Ve vant to tank you and President Rusevelt for to bring us here to America. You save us from hell. God Bless America!"

They all spoke English and I was bored. There were interpreters, but the speeches seemed to go on and on.

We were all sitting on the grassy fields, listening to speeches, chatting in different languages, recalling the stories of internment and escapes. Many were crying. Some just stared blankly into the distance. My mother, holding little

Michael in her arms, and holding Ike's hand, leaned against my father.

"Do you think I will ever hear from, or find any members of my family?" she cried.

"Now that we are in America, we will look for them. There are many organizations which will help us. There are people in the Red Cross, all over the world, dedicated to finding members, and children of the families which were separated. I promise you, we will find somebody," my father reassured her.

In the next few weeks, many Jewish organizations sent representatives to meet the refugees and fill some of their needs. They came to view us like an oddity. Even the people in the town of Oswego came up to the fence and peered in, especially when we arrived. They climbed the trees, piled up in open windows, got on top of the roofs and surrounded the fort. At times, I felt like we were animals in the zoo, there for their entertainment.

The women from Jewish organizations, such as Pioneer Women, started to bring us goodies. They brought baby carriages, bassinets, curtains, blankets, shoes for the kids and many other necessities.

"Here is a beautiful dress for you," one of the women from the Council of Jewish Women from Syracuse, said to me. It was a beautiful blue woolen dress with taffeta lining and brass buttons, with imprinted anchors, which came from the neck all the way down to my knees. It was the most beautiful dress I ever had. I took it and held it close to my body, then put it on over the shirt I was wearing, while the tears ran

down my face. I felt like an American sailor. I felt rich. I knew that in America everything was beautiful. "I think I like this country," I said, out loud to myself.

On the wall of one of the barracks, there was a list of many Jews who escaped and survived the Nazi authorities. Some of the names were followed by the countries they had escaped to. Every morning, my mother's mission became looking at, and reading the names on the list, in hope that some of her sister's or brother's names would appear.

Unfortunately, all her trips were in vain, and her heart would break all over again, every time someone screamed in joy for finding a relative.

Because we came from war torn Europe where many diseases were raging, we were quarantined for 30 days. None of the refugees were allowed out of the fort, and many were upset since they had relatives in the United States who wanted to come and visit them. Their joy at finding each other had to be put on hold for one month. So it was very appropriate when we sang with Bing Crosby and the Andrews sisters, *"Don't Fence Me In."*

In the camp, there was a young man who was a very talented musician, a pianist. Leonce, as we called him. Leon Levitch started a choir for all of us kids. He was a great arranger and composer. He taught us to sing harmony. We learned many American songs, among them were, *"You Are My Sunshine,"* and you could hear the kids all over the camp singing, *"You Are My Sunshine,"* in beautiful harmony. We did many performances, and we all loved it.

Performance at Fort Ontario.

Author - 1st row, 4th from the left.

This was also a time when Bing Crosby serenaded us with, *"I Love You,"* and *"I'll Be Seeing You."* Many people in the camp cried because they wanted to see again, the relatives, who had been massacred by the Nazis, but they all knew that they would never meet again.

One day, when I was in school, after I learned a little English, a girl asked me who did I like better, Bing Crosby or Frank Sinatra. I had never heard of Frank Sinatra, so I told her that I loved Bing Crosby. So, she hit me and ran away.

In the camp, there was a beautiful young woman, whose name was Mania. She was one of the people who performed on the ship. She had a lovely soprano voice.

Mania had a boyfriend that she wanted to marry, but our complicated situation in the camp did not provide for a marriage. They had to take a blood test, and get a license in the city hall of Oswego, but because of the quarantine they could not get out of the camp.

After weeks of waiting and communicating with Washington, the permit was granted and Mania and Ernst were married. This was our first wedding in America. And it was a beautiful wedding on the lawn of Fort Ontario, under the home-made Hupa. Most of the people from the camp came to witness this beautiful occasion.

Mania was born in Germany and she always talked to me in German. I did remember some German from school in Yugoslavia, but she talked so fast, that all I could do was smile, and nod my head. The fact was, that the German refugees wanted all the Fort rules and regulations to be posted in German. The Yugoslavian Refugees wanted

everything posted and spoken in Serbo-Croatian. This became a great cause for dissension. My father, who spoke very little German, would look at them arguing, almost at the point of fists, and could hardly believe the futility of the whole thing.

"Didn't they have enough Hell in Europe? Why are they bringing it here with them?"

Fort Ontario was a cross section of Europe, with different social statuses, different professions, different languages and even different branches of Judaism. The young people seemed to solve this whole problem by speaking Italian. I realized of course, that there will always be a few unhappy people, who with their unhappiness stir up a whole bunch of problems for all of us.

During the time in the Fort, we had English lessons, parties, entertainment and lots of food. To me this felt like one big party. My biggest problem was the language. In my beautiful school in Belgrade, I had studied French and German. At home we spoke Serbo-Croatian and Ladino, (A language peculiar to Sephardic Jews). During the hiding in Italy, I learned to speak Italian, and now I was faced with another new language. The funniest thing though, was watching my family trying to pronounce *the.*

"You have to take your tongue," my uncle would say, " stick it on a table, take a hammer, hit it, and maybe you will be able to say *the.*"

I had a great capacity to learn languages, but this was hard, and it had to be done fast because we were getting ready to go to Public school in Oswego.

In the meantime, we began going to the fence every day to meet the kids from the town.

"My name is Mary Occhino, what is yours?" a sweet little girl approached me through the fence.

"My name, Irena." I said, feeling proud of myself for speaking English.

The people of Oswego, being intrigued by the refugees, started to bring food, clothing, toys and many other things and threw them over the fence for us.

In the meantime, some of the kids dug a hole under the fence by the Lake, crawled through it, and went into town. I never went with them because I knew my father would not approve.

When the time came to go to school, a teacher from the local high school came to the Fort and interviewed all of us kids to see what grade each should be placed in. Even the boy scout leader, Harold Clark, came to the Fort and started a boy scout group for the refugee boys. My brother, Ike, who was about 11, also joined the boy scouts. The boys were very proud, and eager to please and learn. They saved pennies to buy their uniforms. We were all so very grateful for our lives, that we never let anything get in the way of success. We all loved the United States.

For a while, it appeared that we would not be allowed to go to public school. We were not aliens because we were guests of President Roosevelt. We did not come with a visa and we had no status. We were in limbo. I was eager to start school and start learning English. After long debates, the

164

Administration decided, after all, to allow the kids to go to Oswego city school.

My first day in an American school was a disaster. I couldn't understand a word, and didn't know what was going on. The words and the sounds were all the same. I sat in my seat in the classroom and followed the book they were reading. I was frustrated and felt stupid.

In between classes, I saw one of my friends from Fort Ontario. She was reading a book. Her beautiful blond hair draped over half of her face, covering her eye, reminded me of Veronica Lake. My friend, Doris, was very smart, intelligent and well read. I was happy to see her, so I walked over to her

"What are you reading,?" I asked her, trying to connect. In her German conceited self, she looked up from the book and said to me in Italian, "You are too stupid to know, even if I tell you."

I stood there paralyzed. I opened my mouth but nothing came out. I wanted to cry. I wanted to hit her. I wanted to run away, but I just stood there in inertia, looking at her. Little did I know how this statement would influence and affect the rest of my life. In that moment, I felt small, unimportant, stupid and invisible.

She never knew that she was the catalyst to my huge success and all my achievements. For that, I will be grateful to her forever. Ever since that time, I have been very careful what I say, knowing how my words can affect the person I say them to.

To add insult to injury, when I walked into another classroom, the teacher looked at me with disgust.

"Why are you wearing pants to class? Go home and change. This is a school, not a playground."

One of our refugee kids who was already seated translated for me. It was cold, and I wore a warm flannel outfit that an organization gave to me. Needless to say, I went home crying.

There were teachers, and many other people in Oswego, who did not approve of the refugees being brought there. After all, we were there at the expense of taxpayers like herself.

The next day, my little friend, Mary, met me in our Fitzhugh Park school to show me around the classes, and introduce me to a few teachers and different kids.

Even though I did not understand what the words meant, I loved saying the Pledge of Allegiance. I loved looking at the flag of the United States. To me it meant life and freedom. When Mary introduced me to other kids, all I could do was smile. I liked Mary very much. She was sweet and thoughtful. I even invited her to one of the parties in the Fort. I didn't really know what was going on, when we all sat in a circle with a bottle in the middle. A boy spun the bottle. It stopped on Mary and he took her by the hand, into the closet. Everyone was laughing and giggling.

"What is going on?" I asked with curiosity. I was so protected by my parents, that I was very innocent and not knowing.

A few seconds later, the closet door opened and my friend Mary came out crying.

"He was trying to kiss me!" she sobbed. It appeared that she was just as innocent as I was.

I wanted to laugh, but did not want to hurt my friend's feelings. I walked over to her, took her by the hand and we went to the food table. She did come to the Fort again, but not to any more parties. Secretly, I wondered what it would be like to kiss a boy. I wished it had been me in the closet.

My friend Koki, seemed sweet on one of my beautiful girlfriends, Gynette. They started dating, and eventually got married.

Many of the refugee kids were home-schooled during the hiding. They spoke English and fit right into the public schools in Oswego. They took classes in electronics and made little quartz radios. Others took shop and got very close to their teachers. I felt that anything I ever wanted, I had to work hard for. Life never dealt me an easy hand, but I never gave up. No matter how many times I fell down, I picked myself up and moved onward and forward. Failure or resignation was never an option.

Some of the refugees resented not being able to go to town to work, especially since there was a shortage of labor with so many young men from Oswego having been taken into the army. No one in Washington could figure out our status. So no one knew what to do with us. There were no precedents set for people like us.

There were government officials who took advantage of our

uncertain situation. And since they did not like Jews, they used the law as an excuse not to allow us to work. They also tried to send us all back to our countries of origin. It was especially irritating to the refugees, that the German prisoners of war were allowed to work in America and get paid for their labor.

In Europe, the war was nearing the end. The red Armies, under the leadership of Stalin, were beating on the Germans and occupying German Cities. The Red Army, the Communists, were so angry with Germany, that they took revenge on all the German people. They raped women, killed anyone who got in their way, and burned and destroyed whatever was left in the towns. Famine, destruction, desolation and lack of water and electricity, were the rewards Germany reaped at the end of the war, and for many years afterward. We heard that thousands of Germans committed suicide as the end of the war approached because they couldn't stand the thought of not having the Reich.

I had mixed feelings about the situation in Germany. I knew that not all the Germans were Nazis. I knew that there were little girls and boys who lost fathers. I knew that there were mothers losing their sons, however, at the same time I was glad that they were also experiencing the pain of loss such as they inflicted upon us Jews.

The American soldiers, after occupying Germany, entered the concentration camps and crematoriums. I saw pictures that the American soldiers took of those camps. There were huge mounds of nude skeletons. Some, with fear frozen on their skeletal faces. Some covered with caked blood, and some still with eyes open, gaping from their skulls. The American soldiers were horrified with what they found.

Pictures taken by George Brooks. Submitted by his daughter Georgia Farinella.

Retreat Formation in
Adelmanns Felden,
Germany
25 June 45

Photos taken by George Brooks. Submitted by his daughter Georgia Farinella.

Lansberg Concentration Camp
Lansberg, Germany
1945

One American soldier entered a concentration camp and found a girl who was almost dead. He took a candy bar out of his pocket and smeared a little chocolate on her lips. She barely opened her eyes, gave a gentle smile, and closed her eyes again. The soldier cried. She moved her hand and barely touched his, while whispering something in Yiddish. The young soldier was Jewish. He leaned his ear against her lips hoping she would repeat her words, which he did not understand the first time. She stirred feebly, licked her lips and repeated, "I won."

Many years later, I met both of them as they celebrated their wedding anniversary.

After the war, the Americans gathered all the Nazi leaders and made them bury the skeletal bodies. The Americans also made the people from the towns around the camps go in and observe the atrocities committed by their leader. Some Germans declared that they had no idea of what was going on in there.

George Brooks – one of the soldiers who entered the
concentration camps.

Photos taken by George Brooks. Submitted by his daughter Georgia Farinella.

Concentration camp site.

In the months to follow, in Fort Ontario, we had dancing lessons, potato sack races, eggs on a spoon races, and I entered them all, and won many. I had four years to make up for, and I had to try and experience everything that life offered. I didn't just enter the races, I entered to win. I had to prove to myself, and the world, that I was not stupid or a loser. I was a winner, and failure was never an option.

In the camp, there was a boy who played accordion very well. His name was Ernest Spitzer. He also played on the ship when refugees entertained the soldiers. He was cute, and many times I went to bed wondering how it would be to play spin the bottle with him. He did not pay much attention to me, or any other girl. I didn't think he liked me, or even noticed me.

One day there was going to be a party at the club house. I got up in the morning all excited. I could hardly wait to go practice dancing. But to my dismay, when I looked in the mirror I realized that I was covered with a red rash. Of course, the party was out of the question.

"You don't want to give the measles to everyone else at the party," my father said.

"But it can't be measles, I already had the stupid measles," I objected.

A few hours later, the boy I liked came to our door, and asked me to go to the party with him. All I wanted to do was die. Needless to say, he never asked me again, and we never connected.

The winter came, bringing with it dancing snow flakes. At

first it looked beautiful, but when the cold persisted with it's icy fingers tugging at our coats, it became very unpleasant. The icy wind blew from Lake Ontario and Canada.

Our barracks had no insulation, and the cold seemed to come right through the walls which were constructed of two by fours and covered with sheet rock. On the outside, the walls were lined with wooden planks.

My father was in charge of the heating for our barrack. On the first floor there was a room with a very large, hungry furnace. When the January temperature fell into the 20's, he had to feed it every few hours. He would take a big shovel, fill it with coal and feed the monster. There were pipes, leading from the furnace to all of the apartments, which kept us comfortable.

Going to school in the snow was not fun, but it made it all O.K. when on the way we got scoops of ice cream. I had never seen ice cream served or sold in winter. It was delicious, especially the sugar cone. What I liked the best was to watch the beautiful brown chocolate and pink strawberry fall on the white shimmering snow. It made such a beautiful painting.

Oswego was a beautiful little town, especially with a blanket of snow. It looked like a Christmas postcard. Its tree-lined streets reflected the charm of a small American town. The city was divided in two by the Ohio River.

In 1722, the British established a post at the fort and called it Fort Oswego. In 1756, the French forces defeated the British and captured the fort. The first American settlers came to Oswego in 1797. The city of Oswego was incorporated in

1848, shortly after the fort was rebuilt.

One day, I learned that we were going to have a very important visitor. Everyone in the camp rushed around in preparation. I was dying of curiosity. *Was it going to be an American movie star? Maybe Shirley Temple?* I loved to see her tap dance. *Maybe Errol Flynn with his bow and arrow.*

Rachel, the author's mother, upper left, holding the author's brother, Michael

Eleanor Roosevelt in front, facing right.

After a long investigation, I discovered that the visitor was going to be Mrs. Eleanor Roosevelt, the wife of our president. I read that she thought of herself as not being very pretty, but she knew that loyalty and intelligence were going to conquer her physical appearance. She was married to FDR, who was her father's fifth cousin. President Roosevelt's mother did not want him to marry Eleanor and tried to discourage him. But he knew what he wanted. And he wanted Eleanor. Eleanor was 20, and Franklin was 23,

and on March 17th 1905, they became husband and wife. She was very supportive of her husband and was involved in human rights.

Mrs. Roosevelt got out of the limousine and walked down the path of the fort accompanied by the wife of Henry Morgenthau, the Secretary of Treasury. There were no guards, police or detectives. Eleanor was slim and she was regal. After looking at her for a few minutes, all you could see was her kindness and gentleness. Everyone wanted to take a picture with Eleanor Roosevelt.

On April 12th, 1945 President Roosevelt died of a cerebral hemorrhage. His long time friend and lover, Lucy Mercer was by his side. Lucy Mercer was originally hired by Eleanor to be her personal secretary. Their affair started on a day when Eleanor was out of town. Mrs. Roosevelt told her husband to stop seeing Lucy, or she would get a divorce. President Roosevelt's mother thought that a divorce would be detrimental and would kill her son's career. He agreed to stop seeing Lucy, but only verbally.

President Roosevelt was the 32nd president of the United States, and served from 1933 to 1945. He was the only president to serve more than two terms. He took office in the middle of a depression, and was responsible for FDI (Federal Deposit Insurance) and Social Security. It was during his presidency, on Dec 7, 1941, that Japan attacked Pear Harbor, throwing the United States officially into World War ll. President Roosevelt had polio, which left him paralyzed from the waist down. For many years, he hid his disability from his constituents.

When President Roosevelt took office in 1933, the

depression was still rampant in the United States. In 1929, the stock market collapsed and many people committed suicide because they had lost everything. In fact, one of my father's cousins threw himself out of five-story building because he couldn't stand the defeat. The depression had started to correct itself, when America entered the 2nd World War.

I remember when I was nine years old in Belgrade, my father would put on the radio at 3:00 or 4:00 AM and listen to President Roosevelt's speeches, which were simultaneously translated into our language. I don't know, or ever knew then, what he said, but I still remember the sound of his voice. Little did I know, that he would be responsible for my leaving the hell of Europe and coming to America.

When we were selected for the trip to the United States, we all had to sign papers that we would return to our countries of origin after the war ended. With the death of President Roosevelt, we didn't know what was going to happen to us. Harry S. Truman, Roosevelt's vice president, took over the presidency, and Roosevelt missed the victory and the end of war by a few months.

On May 7th, Germany surrendered. The war in Europe was over. Everyone celebrated D Day. In Oswego, all the residents put out flags in front of their houses and waited for their loved ones to return home from the war. But, in the Fort, we, my family, had mixed feelings.

"Where are we going to go?" we kept asking. All of our homes and possessions in the old country were pilfered, stolen or destroyed by Nazis and bombs. All our relatives

were massacred. If we went back, all we would find is death and destruction. But this day, D Day, was for celebration. Hitler was defeated and gone. It was said that he and Eva Braun had taken poison and committed suicide in the their bunker. They got married 40 hours before committing suicide. She was 33, and Hitler was 56.

We all wondered what would happen to Josef Mengele, the German SS officer, and physician, who did experiments on live Jewish children in the concentration camps, which earned him the title of *Angel of Death*. The experiments usually resulted in disfigurement, disability, torture and finally death.

We also wondered what would happen to Adolf Eichmann, the architect of the death camps, and railroads, which took as many as 100,000 Jews daily to death camps to be slaughtered.

"We are going back" my father said. "It will be hard and sad at first, but at least we know the language."

"And, maybe some of my relatives will show up," my mother cried.

On August 6th 1945, we learned of the news that the United States had dropped an atomic bomb, called *Little Boy,* on the Japanese city of Hiroshima, with *Fat Man*, another atomic bomb, to follow on August 9th on the city of Nagasaki. Six days later, on August 15th, Japan surrendered, and on September 2nd, the Second World War was officially over.

Many people condemned President Truman for the atomic

bombs, because the devastation to Japan was incredible. He, however, stated that by ending the war, we saved many American and Japanese soldiers' lives.

With the war being over, we seriously had to consider how to proceed. We were still guests of the president, even though he had died, therefore, we had to abide by the agreement we signed upon entering the United States.

Unbeknown to me, Dr. Ruth Gruber, and a few other refugees were working on getting permission for us to stay in the states. The red tape was incredible. There were the refugee board, Washington administration, Jewish organizations, and many other establishments, all pulling in different directions.

In the meantime, since my father wanted to go back, we started getting our shots and papers in order for our return to Yugoslavia.

Again, I had very mixed feelings. I wanted to go back, but I wanted what we had before the war. I, also, had started to speak a little English, but more than that, I was falling in love with the United States.

My Aunt Erna and Uncle Ralph did not want to go back to Yugoslavia, so they started working on my father to change his mind.

"You want me to change my mind, when we don't even know if we are going to be allowed to stay here," my father said.

My mother did not want to return either. She would do what

my father wanted, but she could not face the fact that her whole family was gone. Of course my father gave in and decided to stay in the USA, if allowed.

Some people were even talking about going to Palestine, the land which God gave to the Jews and which was rightfully theirs, but which they could not access.

The petitions and letters continued going back and forth to Washington regarding our permanent stay in America. Apparently, Truman met with senators, congressmen, the immigration department and many other departments. There were some officials in the government who did not want to open the doors to any refugees, especially Jews. They did not want to set a precedent for letting refugees into the United States.

Dr. Ruth Gruber, and others from Oswego, continued to work tirelessly, and never gave up. Finally, the decision came down to President Truman. He felt such compassion for the people who had been running and hiding for so many years, that he agreed to allow us to stay in the United States.

I think it had nothing to do with Washington, or anything. I think that the Jewish mother, in Dr. Ruth Gruber, just wore him down.

The celebration that went on in the Fort was incredible, especially among the younger people who were planning to go to college and get an education.

Shortly after receiving the news about our staying in America, we were informed that someone was going to come and help us decide where we would make our new home.

We had no relatives in America. We had no jobs here. We had no housing here. We didn't even know the language. There was no government aid, or social security, or unemployment for us. There was nothing.

My mother started to panic. "Where are we going to go? We have no place to go. How are we going to live?" The tears of fear rolled down her face.

My father too was scared, but he did not show it. "We did it during the war, we'll do it again, even better, because now we are free. Here in America, we can become rich and still have a good life."

My Uncle Ralph developed tuberculosis of the spine, as the result of the injury which occurred in the cave during the bombing of Split. He was told that a Jewish Organization in Los Angeles would help him with the hospital bill for a little while and would also find a job for my aunt.

That made it easier for them, because they did not have to make a decision. But my aunt did worry about paying the hospital bills.

"You don't have to worry about it now," my father calmed her. "When the time comes, you'll figure it out."

Of course, he was telling himself not to worry at the same time.

All the refugees waited in line to talk to the agent. He and his table waited for us at the end of the line. I had never seen him before, and he scared me. He did not smile much and didn't seem to be friendly. I wondered if he hated Jews, but

wanted to keep his job. He was going to help us decide where we wanted to go.

Most of the refugees were scared. Those who had relatives in the States knew that they had a place to go to.

As we approached the end of the line, where the inquisitor sat, we heard the people in front of us say Cleveland.

When we reached him, he tried to smile, and he asked us if we had family in the States, or if we knew where we wanted to go to make our new home. All we knew to say was Cleveland, which is what we heard the people in front of us say.

He stuck some papers under our noses, holding the pen he said, "Sign Here."

My brother, Ike, stood there observing. He had learned quite a bit of English, so with a sigh of disgust, he said "Where the Hell Is Cleveland?"

After we said Cleveland, and signed the papers, we couldn't change our minds and go to Los Angeles or New York. So we went to Cleveland, Ohio.

On January 17th, 1946, we were on the bus going to exit and then re-enter the United States legally. Our bus stopped in Syracuse, where Pioneer Women, a Jewish organization, gave us lunch at a Temple.

From Syracuse, New York, we were taken by our bus across the Rainbow Bridge to Ontario Canada, where we signed legal documents, turned around, and through Niagara Falls,

USA, we reentered America, legally.

Five years from that date, we were in Mineola, New York, standing in the courthouse, in front of the Judge.

"Young lady, do you want to become a citizen of the United States of America?"

"Yes, your honor!" I responded with all the enthusiasm I could summon.

"Why do you want to be a citizen?" he asked. His voice was kind, and he had a smile on his face. He reminded me of my father, so he did not scare me.

"Because, I love America!" I exclaimed again, as loud as I could.

"Right answer," he mumbled.

"Can you tell me who was the 16th president of the United States?" he asked, but now his voice was serious.

"Yes, your honor, it was Abraham Lincoln." I responded proudly.

He asked me a few more questions and then congratulated me, making a comment, on how smart I was.

He asked my parents very few questions. Then, I realized that he'd enjoyed playing with me because he loved my enthusiasm. I had a great time, as I usually do.

That day, we were blessed by becoming citizens of the United States of America.

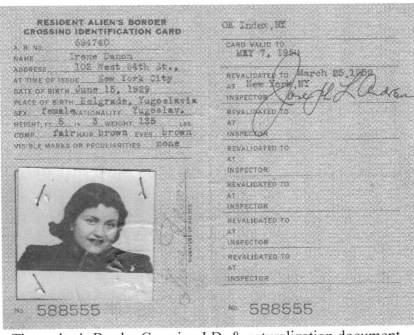

The author's Border Crossing I.D. & naturalization document.

To
Be
Continued...

Appendix

Almost all the young people from Fort Ontario went to school, colleges and universities. Most of them became doctors, scientists, professors and business people.

My parents went into business in Santa Monica, California, bought an apartment house and drove a Lincoln Continental.

My mother found a sister in Israel and flew there to meet with her.

After the death of my husband, I went into real estate, investments and syndications.

We all gave back to this country many times over what the taxpayers invested in bringing us here. We all became proud Americans like the ones that made this county great.

9867182R00125

Made in the USA
San Bernardino, CA
29 March 2014